ROUTLEDGE LIBRARY EDITIONS: JAPAN

THE PHONETICS OF JAPANESE LANGUAGE

I0591696

THE PHONETICS OF JAPANESE LANGUAGE

With reference to Japanese Script

P. M. SUSKI

Volume 59

Routledge
Taylor & Francis Group

LONDON AND NEW YORK

First published in 1931

This edition first published in 2011
by Routledge
2 Park Square, Milton Park, Abingdon, Oxon, OX14 4RN

Simultaneously published in the USA and Canada
by Routledge
711 Third Avenue, New York, NY 10017

Routledge is an imprint of the Taylor & Francis Group, an informa business

© 1931 P. M. Suski

First issued in paperback 2013

British Library Cataloguing in Publication Data
A catalogue record for this book is available from the British Library

ISBN 13: 978-0-415-59413-4 (hbk)

ISBN 13: 978-0-415-85133-6 (pbk)

Publisher's Note
The publisher has gone to great lengths to ensure the quality of this reprint but points out that some imperfections in the original copies may be apparent.

Disclaimer
The publisher has made every effort to trace copyright holders and would welcome correspondence from those they have been unable to trace.

THE PHONETICS OF JAPANESE LANGUAGE

With Reference to Japanese Script

By P. M. SUSKI,

Author of the Dictionary of Kanji

South Pasadena

P. D. and IONE PERKINS

1942

PHONETICS OF JAPANESE LANGUAGE
With Reference to Japanese Script

CONTENTS

Introduction

CHAPTER I
How Japan Acquired the Writing 1

CHAPTER II
Sounds of Kanji 6
  Characters Sounded Alike in Japan and China 12

CHAPTER III
Japanese Sounds of Kanji 15
  Homophonous Characters 17
  Characters Used in Sense Peculiar to Japanese 18

CHAPTER IV
Japan-made Characters & Japan-created Sounds 23
  Kanji Created in Japan 23
  Some Unusual Sounds Peculiar to Japanese 25
  Some Difficult Geographical & Personal Names 25
  Variation in Characters 28

CHAPTER V
Calligraphy 29

CHAPTER VI
Japanese Compositions 32

CHAPTER VII
Japanese Compounds 38
  Japanese Compounds Not Understood by
    Chinese 38
  Meiji Compounds 39
  Examples of Meiji Words 40
  Summary 41

CHAPTER VIII
Phonetic Use of Kanji 43

CHAPTER IX

Kana 45
   I-ro-ha and Gojuin 49

CHAPTER X

ounds of Japanese Speech 55
   Japanese Vowels 56
   Variation in Japanese Vowels 61
   Length of Japanese Vowels 62

CHAPTER XI

Japanese Consonants 66
   T and D 68
   Relation of Z Line to D Line 69
   Y is Shorter and Weaker 69
   Japanese R 70
   Japanese Final N 71
   Contracted or Doubled Consonants 73
   Combined Consonants 76
   Variation in Sounds 77
   Variation According to Time 78
   Individualism and Provincialism 78
   Circumstantial Variations 79

CHAPTER XII

Romaji 80
   Romanized Kana 83
   Japanese System of Romaji 85

CHAPTER XIII

Accents and tresses 89
   Accents on Syllables 90
   Accents on European Languages 91
   Importance of Accents 92
   Peculiarity of Japanese Accents 93
   Elision of Vowels 96

CHAPTER XIV

Japanese Orthography 97
Difficulties of Japanese Orthography 107

CHAPTER XV

Early Japanese Sounds 110
   Influence of Romaji on ounds 113
   General Remarks 114
Errata 116
Glossary 117

INTRODUCTION

The object of this little book is to give true characters of Japanese speech sounds of today in reference to European sounds. So far as I know, there
have been no attempts ever made in this direction,
that is, to record the exact manner in which Japanese sounds are produced. No standard set for sounds,
it is to be presumed that the quality of sounds is
from time to time drifting from one shade to another.

As the writer once wished to learn how Japanese
people used to pronounce when carrying on a conversation 500, 1000, or 1500 years ago, he was utter-
ly disappointed to find nothing giving records of
sounds heard in those remote ages. Phonographs,
which may have served these purposes fittingly are
but an invention of a contemporary.

Japanese vowel elements are only 5 in number
against—English 18, French 13 and German 8.
Japanese consonants are 15, English 26, French 22,
and German 23. Because of the lesser number of
elements, it follows of necessity that the wider
range in vowels and to some extent in consonants
is heard and tolerated by Japanese ears.

This little volume attempts to give average sounds
uttered by Japanese of the present age, in relation
to the English sounds of today, as the latter language is rich in works of phonetics and further-
more is the most widely distributed language of the
world. The English sounds will of course undergo
changes in course of time, as it had in past, as any
other living language. But still there will always

be means to ascertain what are the sounds prevalent in 19th or 20th century, in case our descendants in 30th century, for instance, would try to study them.

As I take English as a standard of measure for Japanese sounds, and I live in America where English is spoken, and as there are more students of Japanese language among English speaking people than any other, and finally there are thousands of American born Japanese who are in need of instruction on true Japanese sounds, this book is written in English language. Japan studies English perhaps more than any one nation studies any one foreign language. Therefore this book can easily find place among records in Japanese libraries.

With the recent perfection of phonographs synchronized with moving pictures, known under various names as Vitaphone, phonocinematography etc., noted speeches of Japanese would become perpetualized. These would corroberate and contribute to the objects of this volume to a great extent. But still a systematized treatise in this subject is a necessity. When a bigger and better text-book on this subject would be written by some future scholars, I would be pleased and satisfied to think this little volume had served as a harbinger.

—P. M. SUSKI.

Los Angeles,
June, 1931.

CHAPTER I

HOW JAPAN ACQUIRED THE WRITING

Whether Japan possessed the art of writing before the introducion of Chinese characters or ideographic script is a matter of conjecture . Letters said to have been found in certain old copies are much like, if not identical, to modern Chosenese alphabet. But the fact that no scripture text had ever been found leads many to doubt the authenticity of such copies.

According to Japanese records, a Korean savant named Wang-in come to Japan during the 16th year of reign of the Emperor Ohjin (285 A. D.) with books of Chinese language and taught the Japanese how to read and write Chinese ideographs. Now this date is believed to be in error by 120 years, which makes it 405 A. D. instead of 285.

At first there seems to have been only a few in the Imperial court that took up learning of Chinese language, but as years go by the study of sounds and meaning of Chinese characters gradually gained ground among the populace. Japanese learners attached to the Chinese characters the meaning in Japanese language, so that each Chinese character has been regarded to have, in addition to the proper Chinese sounds, new Japanese sounds corresponding to the meaning in Japanese.

To illustrate: If England would introduce into the country a Greek word grapho and read it in various ways as grapho, to write, writing, to inscribe, script, inscription, etc., she would be doing exactly what Japan has been and is now doing to the Chinese ideographic script.

The Chinese characters or ideographic writing which were brought to Japan were from the work during the Han dynasty in China. Hence Japanese called them "Kanji" (literally Han characters). They were also known as "Honji" (literally real characters) in contrast to Kana (literally Provisional name).

Some Kanji has two or three different sounds as it had been pronounced in one way during one Chinese dynasty and in another way during another. Most Kanji again were used in two or more different senses in China. Japanese had to learn all these, translated into Japanese. Quite a number of characters, as a result, had to have two or three Chinese sounds and a dozen or more Japanese ways of reading.

The Chinese sounds are known as "on" or "in" (literally: sound) and the Japanese sounds are known "kun", "wakun" or "yomi" (meaning or reading). Among the former are "kan-on" (sounds of Han dynasty) which are by far the most prevalent, "go-on" (sounds of Wu dynasty), and later on "Toh-on" (sounds of T"ang dynasty), "soh-on" (sounds of Sung dynasty), "min-on" (sounds of Ming dynasty) and "shin-on" (sounds of Ts'ing dynasty). The latter four are acquired by Japanese in later period during the intercourse with China, and are limited to only a few characters.

The present day Chinese sounds of characters are widely different from what the Japanese are attaching to the same characters. Moreover, the Chinese sounds vary according to localities in China. The reason why such discrepancies occur are not difficult to understand when we learn that China has undergone a great many changes in dynasties often revolutionary, since Han period when Japanese had been first taught their sounds.

The Han dynasties lasted from 206 B. C. to 220 A.D., then came three kingdoms when Minor Han, Wei and Wu divided the country till 280 A. D., Western Tsin 265-316 A. D., Eastern Tsin 317-420 A. D., the division of the north and south dynasties, each division having four or five courts 386-589 A. D., the reunification of the empire by Sui dynasty 589-618 A. D., T"ang dynasty 618-907 A. D. Five short dynasties 907-959 A. D., Sung dynasties including north and south 960-1279 A. D., Yüan or Mongol dynasty 1280-1368 A. D., Ming dynasty 1368-1644 A.D., and Ts'ing dynasty 1644-1911 A. D. followed in succession.

As a result of such frequent changes in dominating powers, the vast Chinese dominion contains people of widely various origins, different in customs, idioms and sounds of characters. For example, a character meaning man is pronounced in China today as jan, lan, niang, in, jin or yan by the people of Peking, Hankow, Shanghai, Fuhchau, Amoy or Canton respectively.

The sounds of Chinese characters as taught in Japan at the present time and those learned by Japanese 1500 years ago from the continental teachers are supposed to be the same, although we have reasons to suspect that the original Chinese sounds of Han period are largely lost and are substituted by highly Japanized sounds, which would be entirely unintelligible to the Chinese ears, should the people of Han period be given opportunities to hear them.

When a language of one people is learned by another in a large scale, the latter is apt to modify and adapt it to suit his tongue. This fact is exemplified by Japanized English produced through the toil of Japanese students under Japanese teachers during the last half a century.

Shing or tones of Chinese characters never

seem to have been acquired by Japanese, although Japanese poets and a few scholars study a great deal about them.

So the characters or ideographs of the original Chinese language, clad with Japan-modified sounds, some with Japan-created sounds, Japan-invented meanings together with a number of Japan-made characters, became now to be known as Japanese characters, the name of "Kanji" (or Han characters) alone remaining to tell the tale.

CHAPTER II

THE SOUNDS OF KANJI

The method of giving pronunciation to a character in Chinese dictionaries, notably the "K'anghi Tsz'tien", the product during the reign of the Emperor Shêng Tsu Jên (1662-1723) is by means of giving two popularly known characters, the first of which furnishing the initial consonant and the seccond giving the vowel and the final consonant if any. This method is known as Fan Ts'ieh".

In Japan, there are several dictionaries of Kanji patterned after "K'anghi Tsz'tien" of China. They invariably give sounds and Japanese reading in Kana, and also sounds in Fan Ts'ieh. The explanation is also given in classical Chinese.

K'anghi Tsz'tien contains over 45,000 characters, while some of the Japanese dictionaries give nearly 50,000, as they contain all the characters found in K'anghi Tsz'tien and other characters from numerous older sources.

When once Kana is mastered, it is a simple matter to get the correct sound of Kanji in Japanese dictionaries. Older dictionaries give true and correct sounds which are at times different from the popularly accepted sounds of today. Many later dictionaries however give the popular sounds also.

While there are nearly 50,000 characters in largest Japanese dictionaries the actual number of characters ever made use of in Japan may number between 15,000 and 20,-000. It is therefore evident that 30,000 or more have never been used in Japan.

There are, on the other hand, hundreds of Kanji, to which Japanese attached new meanings that have never been so used in China. There are also scores of new characters created by Japanese. Most of these have Japanese sounds or "kun" only and no sounds or "on".

We have 304 varieties of sounds or "on" of Kanji which are in use in Japan. There are many which have two sounds and a few that have three or more.

The variety of sounds of characters in China is much more numerous than that of Japan. Williams' syllabic Dictionary of Chinese Language places the number of Chinese sounds at 522 or 218 more than that of Japanese.

Chinese and Japanese sounds differ widely. But the initial consonants are alike in most cases. The chief difference is in the quality of vowels and endings.

The following is the list of 304 Japanese sounds of Kanji, with an example of each.

阿	a	秒	byoh	鈍	don
哀	ai	謬	byuh	頭	dzu
惡	aku	茶	cha	回	e
安	an	着	chaku	永	ei
軋	atsu	知	chi	益	eki
婆	ba	竹	chiku	延	en
倍	bai	沈	chin	悦	etsu
莫	baku	秩	chitsu	不	fu
挽	ban	貯	cho	風	fuh
伐	batsu	兆	choh	伏	fuku
倍	be	敕	choku	吻	fun
米	bei	蛛	chu	沸	futsu
冪	beki	忠	chuh	賀	ga
勉	ben	椿	chun	害	gai
別	betsu	黜	chutsu	岳	gaku
尾	bi	朶	da	含	gan
敏	bin	臺	dai	合	gatsu
募	bo	濁	daku	外	ge
乏	boh	段	dan	藝	gei
牧	boku	脱	datsu	激	geki
梵	bon	泥	dei	彦	gen
沒	botsu	溺	deki	月	getsu
悔	bu	殿	den	義	gi
分	bun	努	do	吟	gin
佛	butsu	同	doh	互	go
白	byaku	獨	doku	號	goh

獄	goku	北	hoku	各	kaku
艮	gon	奔	hon	甘	kan
具	gu	發	hotsu	割	katsu
遇	guh	百	hyaku	化	ke
軍	gun	表	hyoh	形	kei
瓦	gwa	伊	i	件	ken
外	gwai	域	iki	決	ketsu
丸	gwan	郁	iku	企	ki
逆	gyaku	引	in	掬	kiku
魚	gyo	逸	itsu	斤	kin
業	gyoh	邪	ja	吃	kitsu
玉	gyoku	若	jaku	固	ko
牛	gyuh	自	ji	孝	koh
波	ha	直	jiki	克	koku
敗	hai	軸	jiku	昆	kon
伯	haku	甚	jin	忽	kotsu
制	han	實	jitsu	區	ku
發	hatsu	序	jo	空	kuh
平	hei	上	joh	君	kun
壁	heki	辱	joku	屈	kutsu
片	hen	受	ju	火	kwa
比	hi	什	juh	會	kwai
匹	hiki	熟	juku	擴	kwaku
品	hin	巡	jun	完	kwan
必	hitsu	術	jutsu	活	kwatsu
甫	ho	加	ka	却	kyaku
包	hoh	海	kai	去	kyo

共	kyoh	捏	netsu	林	rin
曲	kyoku	尼	ni	律	ritsu
久	kyuh	肉	niku	路	ro
麻	ma	任	nin	老	roh
每	mai	納	noh	鹿	roku
膜	maku	奴	nu	論	ron
滿	man	若	nyaku	縷	ru
末	matsu	女	nyo	累	rui
命	mei	遶	nyoh	掠	ryaku
免	men	乳	nyuh	慮	ryo
滅	metsu	汚	o	兩	ryoh
味	mi	央	oh	綠	ryoku
民	min	屋	oku	流	ryuh
密	mitsu	音	on	左	sa
茂	mo	乙	otsu	才	sai
毛	moh	羅	ra	朔	saku
沐	moku	磊	rai	山	san
門	mon	落	raku	札	satsu
務	mu	卵	ran	施	se
脈	myaku	辣	ratsu	成	sei
妙	myoh	冷	rei	石	seki
那	na	歷	reki	仙	sen
乃	nai	連	ren	切	setsu
南	nan	列	retsu	車	sha
捺	natsu	利	ri	尺	shaku
侫	nei	力	riki	子	shi
念	nen	陸	riku	弑	shii

式	shiki	泰	tai	腕	wan
叔	shiku	卓	taku	野	ya
心	shin	丹	tan	厄	yaku
失	shitsu	達	tatsu	余	yo
初	sho	帝	tei	用	yoh
小	shoh	適	teki	浴	yoku
食	shoku	天	ten	油	yu
守	shu	轍	tetsu	友	yuh
收	shuh	徒	to	唯	yui
叔	shuku	冬	toh	坐	za
春	shun	得	toku	罪	zai
出	shutsu	屯	ton	斬	zan
素	so	突	totsu	雜	zatsu
双	soh	都	tsu	是	ze
則	soku	通	tsuh	稅	zei
存	son	遂	tsui	善	zen
卒	sotsu	宇	u	絕	zetsu
須	su	云	un	造	zoh
數	suh	鬱	utsu	屬	zoku
水	sui	和	wa	隨	zui
寸	sun	賄	wai		
多	ta	惑	waku		

The vowels a, e, i, o, u are all short except when followed by h, when they are prolonged to double length. The sounds of vowels are explained under the chapter on Romaji.

When two vowels are together as ai, ei,

ii, ui, the quality of each vowel is retained and pronounced successively. No syllable ends with a consonant except n. All sounds consist of one or two syllables. Of two syllable sounds the final syllable is either one of ki, ku and tsu.

The consonants are b, by, ch, d, f, g, gw, gy, h, hy, j, k, kw, ky, m, my, n, ny, r, ry, s, sh, t, w and y. The sound value of these consonants are given in the chapter on Romaji.

Of the 304 sounds here given, there are eight which are no longer distinguished in colloquial speech by majority of Japanese at present. They are gwa, gwai, gwan, kwa, kwai, kwaku, kwan and kwatsu. These are now sounded as ga, gai, gan, ka, kai, kaku, kan and katsu. This cuts down the actual number of sounds to 296.

Some exhaustive Japanese dictionaries give a few other sounds, but they are so extremely rare in actual use, that they are not included in above.

Examples of Some Characters Which Are Sounded Alike in Japan and China

The following are some characters which are sounded in Japan in the same way as in Mandarin Chinese (or Kuan Hua or official Chinese language) of today:

ai	挨靄隘	kwoh	荒皇黃晃恍
chi	知智致值置雉痴遲恥	kyuh	九久究求球救丘臼舅灸糾舊
chuh	注註誅	lai	來賴
chun	蠢	lan	闌蘭藍覽嵐
fu	夫父付敷府訃負	li	李理里梨吏儸履離
i	依伊衣以移遺易異懿縊	lin	吝林臨隣
jun	閏潤	ma	麻馬
kai	開改	mai	埋邁
kan	竿肝干乾敢勘	man	曼滿瞞慢
ki	幾畸基寄紀季旣企冀記起氣奇期欺	min	民
		na	那
		nai	乃
kin	巾今金筋琴近僅謹錦欽禁緊禽	nan	男難南喃
		nu	奴
ku	苦	san	三散
kwa	瓜蝸寡卦	saku	索
kwai	怪拐快	sha	沙砂紗洒
kwan	官冠貫觀寬舘管幹歟灌	shi	仕士矢史尸市氏示始師

shin	辛信新	wi	威爲委韋違
shoh	削		偉圍位謂畏
shuh	羞修囚秀袖		惟胃緯痿維
	須		尉彙
shun	舜	yen	炎烟燕燄焉
			延掩衍厭演
sui	綏碎粹彗		
ta	他	yin	因寅音引印
			淫殷飲胤陰
tai	待	yiu	尤友由又有
tan	丹		右佑祐宥幽
			悠憂優油游
wai	歪		猶遊酉誘
wan	彎	yu	愈諭

The only difference between Japanese and Chinese sounds of characters in this list is as follows: Japanese pronounce r where Chinese sound l.   Japanese omit w and y in syllables wi, yen and yin.

CHAPTER III

JAPANESE SOUNDS OF KANJI

In the study of Chinese ideographic script, what Japanese had done must have been: 1st, to learn form and structure of each character; 2nd, to learn how it is sounded; 3rd, to learn its meaning or what idea does it convey. The meaning translated into Japanese is known as "kun", "wakun" or "yomi", which were actually attached to the corresponding characters so that each character is regarded to have Chinese sounds and Japanese sounds.

Each character has one Chinese sound, only occasionally two or more, but the Japanese sounds are usually numerous, as most characters are used in different senses, the Japanese translation of which naturally varies.

The examples of a few characters with Chinese sounds (as sounded in Japan today), meanings and corresponding J a p a n e s e sounds follow:

Chinese Sound	Meaning	Japanese Sound

北 hoku hai
- north .... kita
- to go north.................... kitasu
- to rebel .... somuku
- to run away.................... nigu
- to defeat .... yaburu

適 teki seki taku chaku
- to suit .... kanau
- to go .... yuku
- incidentally .... tamatama
- ably .... masani
- only .... tada
- heir .... yotsugi

爆 haku hoh boku baku
- to scorch .... yaku
- to dry by fire............ kawakasu
- to crack .... saku

安 an
- easy ....)
- safe ....) yasushi
- cheap ....)
- to pacify .... yasunzu
- why not .... izukunzo

數 shu su saku soku shoku suh
- to count .... kazou
- to measure .... hakaru
- number ....) kazu
- several ....)
- often ....) shibashiba
- frequently ....)

Some characters have only one Chinese and one Japanese sound, as in the following examples:

紙 shi   paper .... kami
海 kai   sea .... umi
林 rin   forest .... hayashi
授 ju   to give .... sazuku
溪 kei   dale .... tani

Homophonous Characters

As in any other language, both the Japanese and Chinese have words sounding the same but having several different meanings. The Chinese characters having the same one sound used for many different senses are given in foregoing examples. Japanese words with one sound but with various meanings may be written with corresponding variety of Chinese characters, are as follows:

Toru in Japanese may mean any one of: to take, to hold, to grasp, to catch, to seize, to get, to rob, to snatch, to occupy, to prefer, etc., and may be written thus:

取 採 捕 把 執 操 攝

Miru may mean: to see, to gaze, to inspect, to experience, to try, etc. Kanji for these are:

見 觀 視 看 睹 瞻

Mata may mean: again, also, twice, etc., Kanji for which are:

又 亦 復

Makotoni may mean: truly, in fact, really, unmistakably, truthfully, faithfully, etc., Kanji for which are:

信 寔 實 洵 眞 誠

Masani may mean: imminently, in response to, squarely, rightfully, obligatory, etc., Kanji for which are:

將 應 方 正 當

Hakaru may mean: to plan, to measure, to survey, to calculate, to confer, to discuss, to compute, etc., Kanji for which are:

圖 度 計 謀 測 量 衡 議

Characters Used in Sense Peculiar to Japanese

While majority of Japanese "kun" given to Chinese characters corresponds to the meaning as used by Chinese people, there are quite a number of instances, where new meanings are attached to Chinese characters by Japanese, different from what Chinese understand them. Thus with some characters, it means one thing in China and an-

other in Japan. With others it means another thing in Japan in addition to what it
means in China. These characters are seldom ever given Chinese sounds or "on".

The examples of this kind of characters
follow:

"on"	"kun"	1st line, meaning in Japan. 2nd line, meaning in China.
佃 --------	tsukada	cultivated land to till ground
偲 --------	shinobu	to reflect on to reprove
伽 --------	togi	attendant a phonetic
俵 hyoh	tawara	straw sack to distribute
倩 --------	tsuratsura	deeply beautiful
偖 --------	sate	so then to tear
劦 --------	shuh	a province united action
坪 --------	tsubo	4 square yards a plateau
壜 --------	bin	bottle a jar

嵐	ran	arashi	storm mist on a hill
抔	-------	nado	and so on to take up with both hands
揃	-------	sorou	to put in order to cut off
杭	-------	kui	a post name of a tree
椎	-------	shii	name of a tree a mallet
様	yoh	sama	condition, polite appellation a pattern*
樋	-------	hi	gutter name of a tree
椿	chin	tsubaki	the camellia a long lived tree
檜	-------	hinoki	Japanese cypress juniper
森	shin	mori	forest luxuriant growth
沖	jun	oki	the open sea to dash against
淋	rin	sabishi	lonesome to pour water

礑	--------	hatato	with a clapping of hand to arrive
磯	--------	iso	a beach a rock
犇	--------	hishi	pushingly to run away
若	jaku	wakai	young to pluck, if*
萩	--------	hagi	the bush clover the mugwort
薄	--------	susuki	marsh grass thin*
膳	--------	zen	food tablet food
臆	oku	omeru	abashed chest, thought
茸	--------	take	mushroom to grow luxuriously
誂	--------	atsurae	to order to play trick
請	sei	uke	to receive to request*
調	choh	shirabe	to investigate to harmonize*

譯	yaku	wake	reason to explain*
賄	wai	makanai	to furnish food wealth
轡	--------	kutsuwa	bridle reins
遉	--------	sasuga	indeed, truly to watch
鍔	--------	tsuba	a sword guard point of spear
鏈	--------	kusari	chain lead ore
霞	ka	kasumi	a haze red clouds
鮎	--------	ayu	the sweet fish the sheat fish
鰹	--------	katsuo	the bonito the black fish
鱶	--------	fuka	shark dried fish

The Chinese meaning which is also understood in Japan is marked with an asterisk.

CHAPTER IV

JAPAN-MADE KANJI AND JAPAN-CREATED SOUNDS

Kanji Created in Japan

Characters created in Japan are not very numerous. Although their use is condemned by scholars of Chinese classics, most of them are in universal use. Naturally they have no Chinese sounds.

佛　omokage (a face)
俥　kuruma (jinrikisha)
働　hataraku (to work)
匁　momme (1 dram)
峠　tohge (a hill)
杣　soma (forest)
桝　maru (square)
杤　tochi (horse chestnut)
柾　masa (grain of wood)
枠　waku (frame)
杢　moku (carpenter)
椚　kunugi (oak)
畠　hata (ranch)
畑　hatake (ranch)
狆　chin (pug dog)
笹　sasa (bamboo)
籾　momi (rice hull)

蓙　goza (straw mat)

碇　shikato (clearly)

裃　kamishimo (kamishimo)

襷　tasuki (tasuki)

蛸　tako (octopus)

躾　shitsuke (discipline)

軈　yagate (soon)

辷　suberu (to slide)

辻　tsuji (cross street)

込　komu (to crowd)

迚　totemo (never)

遖　appare (gloriously)

詫　joh (command)

閊　tsukae (blocked)

雫　shizuku (drops)

鋲　byoh (a tack)

錺　kazari (goldsmith)

鎹　kasugai (cramp)

鰯　iwashi (herring)

鯰　namazu (sheat fish)

鱈　tara (cod fish)

厶	gozaru (is)	糀	kohji (malt)
椙	sugi (fir)	樫	kashi (oak)
鴫	shigi (snipe)	粂	kume
呎	fuhto (foot)	鞆	tomo
吋	inchi (inch)	麿	maro
浬	notto (knot)	噸	ton
碼	yahdo (yard)	磅	pound

Some Unusual Sounds Peculiar to Japanese

Since Kanji has many ways of pronunciation it is extremely difficult to read the Japanese composition. Dictionaries give "on" and "kun", i.e. Chinese and Japanese sounds. But which one is correct for a given place is to be learned by experience only. Sometimes unusual sounds are given to Kanji in compounds of two or more, baffling the learners as they are not to be found in any dictionary. Most of such instances are found among proper names.

Some Difficult Geographical and Personal Names

大和	Yamato	國府津	Kohzu
向日町	Mukohmachi	酒々井	Shisui
笠置	Kasagi	勿來	Nakoso
畝傍	Unebi	足利	Ashikaga
深日	Fuke	動橋	Irugibashi
筋向	Sujikai	石生	Iso
千種	Chigusa	城崎	Kinosaki
燒津	Yaizu	米子	Yonago
石和	Isawa	和氣	Wake
厚狹	Asa	有年	Une
直方	Nokata	鳥栖	Tosu
諫早	Isahaya	飛鳥	Asuka

Some Japanese surnames with unusual pronunciation:

正親町	Ohgimachi	大鋸	Ohga
曾良	Katsura	卜部	Urabe
三枝	Saegusa	床次	Tokonami
萬里小路	Marinokohji	安積	Asaka
敕使河原	Deshigawara	勘解由小路	
日下部	Kusakabe		Kakeyukohji
五十嵐	Igarashi	兩角	Morozumi
百々	Dodo	乙訓	Otokuni
土師	Haji	佐伯	Saeki
刑部	Osakabe, Gyohbu Osabe, Katabe	帶刀	Tatewaki
		宗像	Munekata
		土方	Hijikata
		生方	Ubukata
土生	Habu	弓削	Yuge
御手洗	Mitarai	設樂	Shidara, Shigaraki
支倉	Hasekura		
飛鳥井	Asukai	與謝野	Yosano
幣原	Shidehara	相樂	Sagara
安孫子	Abiko	越智	Ochi
雀部	Sasabe	服部	Hattori
穩田	Onda	渡邊	Watanabe
日置	Hiki	當麻	Taema
行方	Namekata	根來	Negoro
壬生	Mibu		

Among some of the earlier and modern writers are ones who would attach new combination or compounds of Kanji to a colloquial Japanese words. Those words are not legible if not furnished with sound giving Kana. Sometimes Kanji compounds are given sounds in European languages mostly English. These are found especially in technical work.

Japanese compounds other than proper names, which have unusual sounds peculiar to Japanese are not in use so much as formerly. Yet there are quite a number of such compounds are found in popular use, a few examples are therefore given here:

團扇　uchiwa (a round fan)

土産　miyage (a gift, a sovenir)

蒲團　futon (a cushion, a comforter)

日和　hiyori (fine weather)

時雨　shigure (a drizzle)

煙草　tabako (tobacco)

算盤　soroban (abacus)

東雲　shinonome (dawn, day-break)

常盤　tokiwa (evergreen)

流石　sasuga (truly, indeed)

素人　shirooto (amateur)

天晴　appare (admirably, gloriously)

只管　hitasura (urgently, earnestly)

煙管　kiseru (a pipe)

如何　ikan (how)

Variations in Characters

Chinese and Japanese dictionaries give old forms and vulgar forms of some of the characters. Some old forms are just as popularly used in Japan as regular forms while others are obsolete and not recognized any more.

A few comparative examples are given here:

old form
(koji)
華 宍 覩 銕 豊 哥 犇

regular form
(seiji or honji)
花 肉 睹 鐵 禮 歌 奔

popular form
(zokuji)
盖 氷 秘 猫 皐 犲

regular form
(seiji or honji)
蓋 冰 祕 貓 皋 豺

In addition to above are abbreviated form, known as ryakuji. These are, in some cases, of ancient origin, and in others quite modern.

abbreviated form
(ryakuji)
声 仮 沢 尽 辺 旧 耒

regular form
聲 假 澤 盡 邊 舊 來

CHAPTER V

CALLIGRAPHY

By far the most conspicuous among many difficulties the students of Japanese language encounter is the great discrepancy or divergence in forms of Kanji in handwriting from those in print.

Kanji are difficult to master even in print, but the fact that much more contracted, abbreviated or variant forms are frequently used in writing, makes the study quite discouraging to beginners. Kana also are hard to read at times, especially in connected writing.

It is not within the scope of this work to go into details on this subject, but a few facts about styles of writing are given below

The most formal and non-abbreviated form of Kanji, as in ordinary type-print is called shinsho, kaisho, square style or full form. The most abbreviated form is known as soh-sho, running style or grass style. The intermediate form between the two is called gyoh-sho or cursive style.

These three styles are illustrated here.

mincho type	square style	cursive style	grass style
書	書	書	吏
卒	卒	卆	玄
年	年	年	玄
澤	澤	泽	仍
之	之	之	之
流	流	流	协

Characters of modern type-print is a style of "kaisho" presumably created during Ming dynasty, hence the name "Mincho" type. In writing "kaisho," the form in the second column is the rule, although some abbreviation and alteration make it look different from the type-print. This style is used in most formal occasion. The cursive and grass styles are used mostly in ordinary writing.

The ancient style "tensho," often called "seal characters," because of its use almost exclusively for seals at the present time, is sometimes very difficult to read. Another old style "reisho," which is of later creation than "tensho," is more easily legible. This style is now often seen on signboard or monument.

The art of writing called "calligraphy" is much cultivated in Japan as well as in China, and masters of renown appeared from time to time in both countries. Writing by some of the masters on a sheet of paper is often valued at many thousand dollars as a work of art.

CHAPTER VI

JAPANESE COMPOSITIONS

Although the study and practical application of Chinese characters into daily life in Japan become general in course of a comparatively short time after their introduction to Japan, it is remarkable that the Japanese syntax did not become modified thereby.

The normal Japanese grammatical order of subject—attribute—predicate and the preposition after the word it governs, has been always retained even when reading classical Chinese sentences, by jumping back and forth from word to word.

Chinese classical sentences (known as "Kanbun" in Japan) were composed by Japanese according to rules of Chinese syntax, but the reading was invariably done according to the Japanese grammar. It is universally practiced to put signs and figures (called kaeriten) to show orders in reading, especially for the benefit of beginners.

The following are examples of a Kanbun or classical Chinese sentence composed by a Japanese writer, the first without and the second with reading signs, known as "kaeriten." The third is written in Japanese reading order with the help of Kana mixed between Kanji. This kind of composition is called "kana-majiri bun." The fourth which is the popular form appearing in newspapers and magazines, gives direc-

tions how to read kana along side and between Kanji.   Kana at the side of a Kanji is
called "furigana."

Normal Japanese and Chinese method of
writing is to begin at top and run downward,
the next line following to the left and so on.
Hence a book begins at where English book
ends.

In this book, quotations from text, as examples here, are given in Japanese manner,
that is in vertical lines.   Only where individual characters are given mixed with
English characters, they are made to run
sideways.

The example taken is a passage from
"Chuchoh Jijitsu" and is given in four different styles.   1. Straight Chinese characters
with punctuation.   2. The above, with reading directions.   3. In Japanese order mixed
with kana.   4.The same with sounds in
kana along side Kanji.   The last two are
styles seen in most Japanese books, newspapers and magazines at present.

The following should be read with the page
held so that the right hand edge comes to
bottom, beginning at top of the right hand
end line, reading down.   Other examples
following are read in the same manner.

博覽以文神武周公孔子之大聖亦興中州往古之神
欲以文之湯帥禹古聰子帝往而太五州武籍皇中聖典
三興帝讚朝亦神仁外聖應王凡大字微也之漢事籍子
知之漢孔始國達公州外通周中通能武

聖共揆一也。故讀其書則其義通。無所間
隔其趣向淘合符節。採挹斟酌則又以足
補助王化矣。

中州始知漢字。應神帝聖武而聰達。博
欲通外國之事。徵王仁讀典籍。大子博
師之。以能通達漢籍也。凡外朝三皇五
帝禹湯文武周公孔子之大聖亦與中州
往古之神聖共揆一也。故讀其書。則其
義通無所間隔其趣向淘合符節。採挹
斟酌則又以足補助王化矣。

中州始めて漢字を知る、應神帝聖武にして聰
達、博く外國の事に通ぜんと欲し、王仁を徵し、
典籍を讀ひ太子之を師とし以て能く漢籍に通
達せり、凡そ外朝三皇五帝禹湯文武周公、
孔子の大聖も亦中州往古の神聖と共揆一なり、
故に其書を讀まば則ち其義通じて間隔する所な
し、其趣向は符節を合するが如し、採挹斟酌則
ち又以て王化を補助するに足る矣、

中州始めて漢字を知る、應神帝聖武にして聰
達博く外國の事に通ぜんと欲し、王仁を徵し、

漢籍に通じ、能く以て師とし讃む。太子之を師とし、凡そ外朝三皇五帝禹湯文武周公孔子の大聖も、亦中州往古の神聖と共に揆を一にするなり。故に其書を讀まば則ち其義通じ、聞隔する所なし。其趣向は猶符節を合するが如し。抉摘斟酌すれば則ち又以て王化を補助するに足るなり。

If Japan had adopted the way of reading these sentences as Chinese do, that is to read straight down in "on" or sounds only, (in Japanes sounds) it would be like the following:

Chuhshuh shi chi Kanji, Ohjin tei seibu ji sohtatsu, haku yoku tsuh gwaikoku shi ji, choh Wani toku tenseki, taishi shi shi, i noh tsuhtatsu Kanseki ya, han grawichoh Sankwoh Gotei U Toh Bunbu Shuhkoh Kohshi shi taisei eki yo chuhshuh ohko shi shinsei ki ki itsu ya, ko toku ki sho, soku ki gi tsuh, mu sho kankaku, ki shukoh yuh goh fusetsu, saiyuh shinshaku, soku yuh i soku hojo wohkwa i.

But, as a matter of fact the above mode of reading had never been practiced by Japanese, in all probability because it was too difficult to master Chinese "shing" or intonation which is something entirely new to Japanese ears and tongue, and yet it is essential in understanding the passage. Without "shing," the Chinese monosyllables will become ambiguous.

In Japan, all four sorts of writing are invariably read in the following manner:

Chuhshuh hajimete Kanji wo shiru. Ohjintei seibu ni shite sohtatsu, hiroku gwaikoku no koto ni tsuh zento hosshi, Wani wo meshi tenseki wo yomu. Taishi kore wo shi to shi motte yoku Kanseki ni tsuhtatsu seri. Oyoso gwaichoh Sankwoh Gotei U Toh Bunbu Shuhkoh Kohshi no taisei mo mata chuhshuh ohko no shinsei to sono ki itsu nari. Yue ni sono sho wo yomaba sunawachi sono gi tsuhji, kankaku suru tokoro nashi, sono shukoh was fusetsu wo gassuru ga gotoshi. Saiyuh shinshaku sunawachi mata motte wohkwa wo hojo suru ni taru i.

The following example is taken from the Chinese classic, "The code of filial piety." How Chinese in different localities read it and how Japanese would read it if the Chinese method of reading in "on" only were followed, are given side by side.

Then follows the same passage with Japanese reading signs as seen in books published in Japan, and the Japanese way of reading the same.

夫孝者天之經地之義民之行也人不知孝父母獨不
思父母愛子之心乎

Kuan Hua, (Mandarin or official Chinese)

Fu hiao, t'ien chi king, ti chi i, min chi
hing ye, jan puh chi hiao fu mu, tuh puh sz'
fu mu ngai tsz chi sin hu.

Canton dialect,

Fu hao che, t'in chi king, ti chi i, man chi
hang ya, yan pat chi hao fu mo, pat sz' fu
mo oi tsz chi sam u.

Amoy dialect,

Hu hau chia, t'ien chi keng, te chi gi, bin
chi heng ya, jin put ti hau hu bo, tok put su
hu bo ai chu chi sim ho.

Japanese in "Kan-on,"

Fu koh sha, ten shi kei, chi shi gi, min shi
koh ya, jin fu chi koh fu bo, doku fu shi fu
bo ai shi shi shin ko.

But Japanese would never read the above
passage in this manner.

The same text, when published in Japan
would always bear reading marks as in the
following:

夫孝者天之經'地之義'民之行也°人不ㇾ知ㇾ孝三父
母'獨不ㇾ思ㇾ父母愛ㇾ子之心ㇾ乎°

Japanese would invariably read this passage thus:

Sore koh wa, ten no kei, chi no gi, tami
no okonai nari, hito fubo ni koh naru wo
shirazu, hitori fubo ko wo ai suru no kokoro
wo omowazaran ka.

CHAPTER VII

JAPANESE COMPOUNDS

The Japanese had to study both the Chinese and the Japanese grammars; the Chinese grammar to understand or write Chinese classics and the Japanese grammar to read the Chinese composition in Japanese way and to write Japanese composition.

Order of words is often the opposite in Chinese and Japanese syntaxes, but in many compounds of two or more characters, the Chinese order of characters is retained in written as well as in spoken Japanese, as is shown by following examples. Today the Chinese order of characters for these examples is popularized in Japan.

讀書'作文'禁酒'懷舊'求道'惜別'不審' 未曾有

所爲'所謂'就中'所以'消火器'擧手禮'停車場

傲兵令'不可思儀'不得要領'傍若無人'徹頭徹尾

Japanese Compounds Not Understood by Chinese

New compounds taking two or more Kanji have been from time to time, created in Japan. These compounds, though composed of Chinese characters are not understood by Chinese. Some of them are:

法印´　沙汰´　披露´　振舞´　文´　起請文´　方´味´手´　斟酌´　島´敏´
用心´　名代´　見参´　相談´　對面´　騷動´　等´　郎砲´　鐵
撩治´　畢竟´　假初´　奉行´　器量´　病氣´　無理´　約束´
有様´　武藝´　挨拶´　愚痴´　出頭´　人間´　師匠´　相續´
言語同斷　不自由´　律義´　至極´　頑固´　警固´　遠慮´　世間´

Meiji Compounds

After the Meiji restoration in 1868 Japan took in western civilization under the guidance of Europe and America. New things came to Japan in wholesale scale, in forms of railways, telegraphs, army and navy, laws, postal service, government, education, agriculture, medical science, commerce and banking, industry and machinery, philosophy and literature, religions, art, sculpture and painting, and revolutionized the mode of living of the people in every way.

With new things, new terms for them to be created in Japanese language were necessary outcome. Thousands and thousands of these newly coined words, which gradually came into use, are composed, in most cases of compounds of two Kanji.

Yukichi Fukuzawa, the founder of Keio Gijuku, the forerunner of the present Keio University, who wrote a book describing his tour of Europe and America is responsible for a great many of these new terms.

It can be safely said that the words used

by Japanese today in writing and conversation are mostly those which were created during Meiji era.

Examples of Meiji Words

西洋　平民　士族　開拓　議會　憲法　帝國　内閣

銀行　新聞　電話　電信　郵便　汽船　汽車　東洋

自動車　自轉車　人力車　馬車　自由　通信　印刷

條約　租借　特權　關係　談判　教育　學校　電車

材料　再版　工業　檢査　建築　裁判　債券　細胞

權利　採集　原籍　歳入　製造　軍隊　健康　現在

代言　會社　後見　國際　國會　豫算　速記　縣廳

詳細　合理　熱心　注意　整頓　普及　蓄積　令孃

名譽　召集　主任　行政　滿足　成功　地理　精神

車夫　活動　合格　頭取　招待　修辭　交換　道德

卒業　世界　社交　消化　勉強　傍聽　前提　除外

品行　熟練　結果

Chinese people would not readily understand the meaning of these new Japanese terms, although they understand the meaning of component characters individually. They have their own compounds different from those of Japanese. But modern tendencies are, that these Japan-made compounds are gradually finding places in Chinese books and newspapers. Thus Japan borrowed the characters from China 1500 years ago, and is now returning them to China in form of compounds.

Summary

So far we have seen how Chinese ideographic script, which is called Kanji by Japanese were introduced to Japan. The sounds and meanings of its characters were studied.

In Japanese adaptation, Kanji were sounded as Chinese did in some cases and read in Japanese meaning in others, so that now one character has "on" and "kun" or Chinese and Japanese sounds. The Japanese sounds are usually many for one character.

The "on" or sounds supposed to have been taught from Chinese became simplified and the Japanese at present distinguishes 304 different sounds while Chinese of today have 522 sounds.

Japan abolished the "shing" by which Chinese distinguishes fine shades of sounds and intonations.

Japanese attached new meanings to some characters. Some new characters were also made by Japanese. Japan also learned various styles of writing.

Japanese did not adopt Chinese grammar except to compose classical Chinese sentences. They never read them straight down in Chinese fashion, but always resorted to the back and forth reading to conform to the Japanese grammar.

Japanese composition is nothing but the classical Cninese rewritten in order according to Japanese grammar, supplanted with kana between where necessary to facilitate the reading.

A great many Japanese compounds were coined in Japan from time to time. During Meiji era when western civilization came in in a large scale, thousands of new compounds were created. These are now being reimported into Cnina.

CHAPTER VIII

PHONETIC USE OF KANJI

Soon after the introduction of Chinese characters into Japan, the Japanese who had already old myths, religion, literature and history in unwritten traditions, commenced to utilize Chinese characters in recording them into writing. In doing so, however, they had to, at times, resort to write Kanji for phonetic value only, disregarding the inherent meaning of characters, especially for proper names and other things which have no parallel in China.

Thus, Kanji were employed in two different purposes, viz. the first, in the same manner as were used in China and the second for phonetic value only, entirely disregarding the meaning. In ancient Japanese literature as "Kojiki" (written early in 8th century) and in still older "Norito" or Shintoh rituals, Kanji are employed in these two different ways mingled together. The general text of Kojiki is written in classical Chinese, but the Norito is written in Japanese reading order.

Poems in Kojiki and Man-yoh-shuh (or Book of Milliard Leaves) are written with Kanji for phonetic value only, though in the latter there are few Kanji used for their own meanings. Phonetic use of Kanji is based primarily on the sounds or "on", but a few are based on "kun" or Japanese sounds.

The following are examples of poems from sources above mentioned:

夜久毛多都°伊豆毛夜幣賀岐°都麻碁微爾°夜幣
賀岐都久流°會能夜幣賀岐夜遠°

Yakumo tatsu, itsumo yaegaki, tsuma-
gomeji, yaegaki tatsuru, sono yaegaki o.

阿米都知能°等母爾比佐斯久°伊比都夏等 許能
久斯美多麻°志可斯家良斯母°

Ametsuchi no, tomoni hisashiku, iitsu-
geto, kono kushi mitama, shakashi
kerashimo.

田子之浦從°打出而見者眞白衣°不盡能高嶺爾°
雪波零家留°

Tago no ura yu, uchiidete mireba,
machiro ni zo, fuji no takane ni, yuki
wa furikeru.

The first example is a poem from Kojiki,
the second from Man-yoh-shuh. These two
consist entirely of characters used phonetically. The third which is also from Man-
yoh-shuh is a mixed one. The 4th, 6th, 7th,
9th, 11th, 12th, 17th, 18th, 20th and 22d
characters are used for their inherent meanings and the rest for phonetic value.

A composition which is a mixture of Kanji
for their own meaning and those for phonetic value is the forerunner of the Japanese
composition of today, in which the phonetic
Kanji is differentiated by simplification of
form. The simplified phonetic characters
are "kana" of today. A sentence composed
of Kanji and kana is a kana-mixed sentence
or "kanamajiri bun", the standard form of
writing in Japan, today.

CHAPTER IX

KANA

Kanji used for phonetic values are known as "kana". Such kana as appearing in Kojiki, Man-yoh-shuh and other ancient scripture are regular Kanji and are called "Man-yoh-gana".

It seems that many different Kanji served to represent one and the same sound. The number of different sounds thus represented by Kanji is forty-seven, but the characters used phonetically may number over three hundred. These Kanji serving as kana were in time written more and more in abbreviated running style, until they developed into "hiragana".

There are two different styles in hiragana. One is the ordinary hiragana of today, having one form for each sound, and the other is "hentaigana" or variants comprising various forms for the same one sound. The use of hentaigana has been in vogue before Meiji era.

The "katakana" is another form of kana, very seldom used before Meiji, but is in extensive use today. It consists of a part of Manyoh-gana characters.

The following table gives the more important Manyoh-gana, hentaigana alongside with each of hiragana and katakana of today with sounds in Romaji.

Manyoh-gana	Hentaigana	Hiragana	Its Probable Origin	Katakana	Its Probable Origin	Romaji
伊以意移		い	伊	イ	伊	i
呂路露樓漏		ろ	呂	ロ	呂	ro
波半者八葉顔婆盤		は	波	ハ	八	ha
爾邇仁丹兒耳二		に	仁	ニ	二	ni
保本穗報寶菩番蕃品富		ほ	保	ホ	保	ho
皿遍篇幣倍邊平反閉		へ	邊	へ	邊	he
止登東度斗等刀		と	止	ト	止	to
知地千遲智		ち	知	チ	千	chi
利里李理梨離		り	利	リ	利	ri
奴努怒弩		ぬ	奴	ヌ	奴	nu
留流琉累類		る	留	ル	流	ru
遠袁越乎		を	遠	ヲ	乎	o
和丸王倭		わ	和	ワ	和	wa
加可果閑嘉香我賀歌迦訶甲駕		か	加	カ	加	ka

Manyoh-gana	Hentaigana	Hiragana	Its Probable Origin	Katakana	Its Probable Origin	Romaji
與代余豫用餘		よ	與	ヨ	與	yo
多當堂太他		た	太	タ	多	ta
禮連麗		れ	禮	レ	禮	re
曾楚所處則宗蘇		そ	曾	ソ	曾	so
川都津通徒		つ	川	ッ	川	tsu
禰年然尼泥		ね	禰	ネ	禰	ne
奈那南難		な	奈	ナ	奈	na
良羅樂		ら	良	ラ	良	ra
武牟無舞无		む	武	ム	牟	mu
字有雲汗		う	字	ウ	字	u
井爲位遺韋		ゐ	爲	ヰ	井	i
乃能農濃廼		の	乃	ノ	乃	no
於意隱游		お	於	オ	於	o
久玖九具供		く	久	ク	久	ku
也夜屋邪		や	也	ヤ	也	ya
末万萬眞滿麻磨		ま	末	マ	末	ma
計个希祁稀氣遣		け	計	ケ	个	ke

Manyoh-gana	Hentaigana	Hiragana / Its Probable Origin	Katakana / Its Probable Origin	Romaji
不布婦賦	*(handwritten)*	ふ 不	フ 不	fu
己古故許去胡	*(handwritten)*	こ 己	コ 己	ko
江衣盈要兄愛	*(handwritten)*	え 江	エ 江	e
帝天亭轉傳	*(handwritten)*	て 天	テ 天	te
安阿	*(handwritten)*	あ 安	ア 阿	a
左佐沙散斜	*(handwritten)*	さ 左	サ 草	sa
幾支喜起木貴岐紀吉伎	*(handwritten)*	き 幾	キ 幾	ki
由遊油游弓	*(handwritten)*	ゆ 由	ユ 弓	yu
女米兔面馬妙賣	*(handwritten)*	め 女	メ 女	me
三美見身微禰味	*(handwritten)*	み 美	ミ 三	mi
志四事新之芝師斯紫色	*(handwritten)*	し 之	シ 之	shi
惠衛繪	*(handwritten)*	ゑ 惠	ヱ 慧	e
比飛非肥日悲	*(handwritten)*	ひ 比	ヒ 比	hi
毛母茂裳	*(handwritten)*	も 毛	モ 毛	mo
世勢齊聲	*(handwritten)*	せ 世	セ 世	se
寸春須壽州數	*(handwritten)*	す 寸	ス 須	su
		ん 无	ン	un

The last kana, although not found in older books and therefore must be of recent invention, plays an important role in modern Japanese syllabary as its use at present is as frequent as any other kana. Formerly mu used to be used in its place. Whether it has been pronounced mu or n is not clear.

All Japanese kana in Romaji are given again below:

i ro ha ni ho he to chi ri nu ru o

wa ka yo ta re so tsu ne na ra mu u

i no o ku ya ma ke fu ko e te a

sa ki yu me mi shi e hi mo se su un

I-ro-ha and Gojuin

The above is the standard order of Japanese syllabary, called "iroha" after the first three syllables, in the same fashion as the English alphabet is called A B C or Greeks called it—alpha-beta. Iroha is said to have been first arranged by Kobo-Daishi (774-834 A. D.) in a poem which reads:

Iro wa nioedo
　　chirinuruo,
Wagayo tarezo
　　Tsune naran?
Ui no okuyama
　　Kyoh koete,
Asaki yume miji
　　Ei mo sezu.

Chamberlain's translation is as follows:

Though gay in hue,
The blossoms flutter down,
    Alas! who, then in this world of ours,
May continue forever?
    Crossing today the utmost limits
Of phenomenal existence,
    I shall see no more fleeting dreams,
Neither be any longer intoxicated.

It is presumed that Kobo-Daishi arranged this poem using each of all Japanese sounds once and leaving none out. But the modern Japanese pronounce we, wi and wo exactly like e, i and o respectively, which makes repetition of same sound in three cases. It may be surmised that the Japanese of former days had sounds for we, wi and wo different from those for e, i and o.

It is also to be noticed that some of aspirate consonants in modern "iroha" are vocalized in Kobo's poem. All h are silent and converted to w before a, two syllables combine to make another sound in one place.

Dots and circles are added to some kana to modify sounds, but these signs are not to be seen in older books. They must be therefore of later invention. Ancients have been vocalizing syllables where required for the sake of euphony.

The aspirate consonants vocalized through addition of double dots are k, s, t and h. It is peculiar that Japanese considered h to be apirate, whose corresponding vocal consonant to be b and its contracted or compressed form to be p; whereas phonetically considered we know p is an aspirate and b is its vocal form, and has nothing in relation with h, which is of entirely different construction.

Dots and circles are not omitted any more where required since Meiji era. Difficulties concerning where to vocalize or compress are thereby eliminated. The only remaining difficulties are in where to pronounce h and where not and where to combine two or more kana to make a new sound and where not.

Writing in Romaji avoids these difficulties as it directly represents what is sounded. But what is written in Romaji cannot be readily converted into kana writing, without thorough knowledge of Japanese orthography, a rudiment of which is given in chapter XIV.

The modification of kana sounds by dots or circles is best explained after giving another arrangement of kana called "Gojuin" or "Fifty Sounds." This arrangement is more modern and scientific. It is based on five vowels in a group and nine consonants combining with each of vowels in order. It is really a phonetic arrangement.

	a column	i column	u column	e column	o column
a line	a	i	u	e	o
k line	ka	ki	ku	ke	ko
s line	sa	si	su	se	so
t line	ta	ti	tu	te	to
n line	na	ni	nu	ne	no
h line	ha	hi	hu	he	ho
m line	ma	mi	mu	me	mo
y line	ya	yi	yu	ye	yo
r line	ra	ri	ru	re	ro
w line	wa	wi	wu	we	wo

Some of these however do not correctly represent the Japanese sounds of today. The second and the third syllables of t line are more like tsi and tsu. The second and the fourth syllables of y line are sounded and written like those of a line. The third syllable of w line is also sounded and written like the third syllable of a line. The second, the fourth and the fifth syllables of w line are written different from but sounded exactly like those of the a line.

Modern Romaji therefore represents kana sounds with the following:

a	i	u	e	o
ka	ki	ku	ke	ko
sa	shi	su	se	so
ta	chi	tsu	te	to
na	ni	nu	ne	no
ha	hi	fu	he	ho
ma	mi	mu	me	mo
ya	i	yu	e	yo
ra	ri	ru	re	ro
wa	i	u	e	o

The name, "Fifty Sounds" is a misnomer. There are only forty-four sounds and the number of kana characters is forty-seven.

The second syllable of s line is written shi and the third syllable of h line is written fu for reasons given under sounds of Japanese consonants.

The modification of kana by dots or vocalization of aspirate consonants affects the syllables of k, s, t and h lines, resulting in production of g, z, d and b lines. The modification by compression of h line produces p line.

ga	gi	gu	ge	go
za	ji	zu	ze	zo
da	ji	zu	de	do
ba	bi	bu	be	bo
pa	pi	pu	pe	po

Here again irregularities analogous to those in aspirate consonants are seen. Those sixty-seven varieties of sounds of kana together with final n, making sixty-eight in all, constitute the total elements of modern Romaji. The number of different kana characters is seventy-three. In other words, Japan has seventy-three kana characters, including modifications by addition of dots and circles, but no more than sixty-eight sounds.

These sixty-eight kana sounds may be called single sounds, as each of them can be represented with a single kana. But in practical Japanese speech, are heard thirty-three other sounds which may be called combined or compound sounds. They can be inadequately representable with combination of two or more kana characters, without however any means to show that the sounds are to be combined into one, instead of sounded separately. The compound sounds are here given in Romaji with usual kana combinations inclosed in brackets:

kya	(ki-ya,	ki-a),	kyu	(ki-yu,	ki-u),	kyo	(ki-yo,	ki-o)
sha	(shi-ya,	shi-a),	shu	(shi-yu,	shi-u),	sho	(shi-yo,	shi-o)
cha	(chi-ya,	chi-a),	chu	(chi-yu,	chi-u),	cho	(chi-yo,	chi-o)
nya	(ni-ya,	ni-a),	nyu	(ni-yu,	ni-u),	nyo	(ni-yo,	ni-o)
hya	(hi-ya,	hi-a),	hyu	(hi-yu,	hi-u),	hyo	(hi-yo,	hi-o)
mya	(mi-ya,	mi-a),	myu	(mi-yu,	mi-u),	myo	(mi-yo,	mi-o)
rya	(ri-ya,	ri-a),	ryu	(ri-yu,	ri-u),	ryo	(ri-yo,	ri-o)
gya	(gi-ya,	gi-a),	gyu	(gi-yu,	gi-u),	gyo	(gi-yo,	gi-o)
ja	(ji-ya,	ji-a),	ju	(ji-yu,	ji-u),	jo	(ji-yo,	ji-o)
bya	(bi-ya,	bi-a),	byu	(bi-yu,	bi-u),	byo	(bi-yo,	bi-o)
pya	(pi-ya,	pi-a),	pyu	(pi-yu,	pi-u),	pyo	(pi-yo,	pi-o)

CHAPTER X

SOUNDS OF JAPANESE SPEECH

It would seem, in a book titled Phonetics, too much space was given to preliminary statements about written Japanese, before we come to chapters or phonetic analysis of Japanese sounds.

But really it was a necessity to describe how Japanese sounds are outcome of Chinese sounds and ancient Japanese; the language itself is based, not on spoken tongue but rather on written words, which allow varied sounds, circumstantial or personal. Relation of written characters to sounds is not like that of other languages. Romaji is a fairly good representation of spoken Japanese, but it is not yet universally adopted, and besides there are varieties of Romaji systems.

For years movements are on to replace phonetic alphabetical script for difficult Kanji, but so far Kanji mixed with kana is the official mode of writing.

Considering all these points, it was deemed advisable to present what is the status of Japanese language today by giving space to the subject in chapters heretofore. Then we feel well prepared to analyze sounds of Japanese language.

Japanese Vowels

The division of sounds into two classes, namely, vowels and consonants is of European origin. No mention has ever been made in older Japanese books of pre-Meiji era. It is only after western ideas were introduced into Japan, that the analysis of sounds into vowels and consonants is made. Some such terms as father-sound, mother-sound, and child-sound were mentioned in some books of Meji period. But there is no way of telling whether those were translation of western phonetic terms. In any case, sounds of Japanese language can be classified into vowels and consonants, even if there are no characters to represent vowels and consonants separately.

Now let us consider Japanese vowels which are five in number in relation to English vowels. Commencing with a high-front-tongue vowel as e in be, continue to utter a sound gradually lowering the tongue and jaw until the sound assumes the quality of a in art, then recede the tongue backward, at the same time round the lips until the sound produced will be that of u in rude, all in one breath of voice; the sounds of all vowels given below will have been produced with all shades of possible vowel sounds between each successive two.

e in be
i in it
a in fate
e in egg
e in there
a in at
a in art
a in all
u in up
o in odd
o in oak
u in put
u in rule

The movements of the tongue, jaw and lips without jerks or stopping and with a continued uniform utterance of voice will take an exercise for a number of times. The whole operation from e to u should not take any more than five seconds.

The relative positions of Japanese vowels will be at points as indicated in the diagram below:

e in be	i in it	a in fate	e in egg	e in there	a in at	a in art	a in all	u in up	o in odd	o in oak	u in put	u in rude
e	i	a	e	e	a	a	a	u	o	o	u	u
イ		エ			ア				オ			ウ

In English vowels further differentiation and subdivision can be made, thus: e in be is more close than e in react, a in educate is more open than a in fate. The same sort

of subdivision can be made with most of
other vowels. The vowels in accented syllables are, in general, more teuse, high, narrow or close than those in unaccented syllables. Only thirteen typical English vowels
are given in above table, but in reality there
are more.

Japanese vowels, on the other hand, are
limited to only five, distributed along English vowel scale at fairly uniform distances.
It is natural that a rather wide latitude is
allowed to the quality of each vowel. In
fact, close or open, front or back variety of
Japanese vowels is considered as a personal
or provincial difference. So, there is hardly
any difficulty in understanding the speaker
on that account. Japanese ears can toler-
ate a considerable range in quality of vowel
sounds.

Only thing, however, concerning the manner in which average Japanese would utter
his vowel sounds is very important and
needs a mention here. Japanese as a whole,
almost invariably moves the mouth, tongue
and jaw in speech much less than people
speaking English, French, German or any
other European languages.

After a series of observations on various
subjects including Japanese, American and
German people, the results given below are
obtained.

When a Japanese would pronounce a i u e o
in succession, the distances between edges

of teeth, between lips and between corners
of mouth will be as follows:

	distance between teeth	distance between lips	distance between corners of mouth
a	1/16 inch	¼ inch	2 inches
i	1/32 inch	¼ inch	2 inches
u	1/32 inch	1/16 inch	1½ inches
e	1/16 inch	¼ inch	1¾ inches
o	1/16 inch	¼ inch	2 inches

Whereas if an average American would
pronounce ah, ee, oo, ay, oh in succession, the
distances between teeth, between lips and
between corners of mouth would show following measures:

ah	½ inch	1 inch	2 inches
ee	1/16 inch	½ inch	2¼ inches
oo	¼ inch	⅛ inch	¾ inch
ay	¼ inch	1⅛ inches	2 inches
oh	⅜ inch	⅜ inch	1¼ inches

Of course in actual speech, both in Japanese and American, variations from the measures given here are liable to occur, according to the expression, loudness of speech,
emotion or degree of excitement; but the
general tendency of Japanese to pronounce
with less movements of mouth parts in
speech is distinctly observable.

As a general rule it is not of absolute necessity to open jaws or lips to a fixed degree to utter a given sound. Ventriloquists are trained to pronounce vowels of open or closed quality at will, without seeming movements of lips or jaws. The volume of mouth cavity may be, upon training, changed to a required size at will, without visible movements of lips. Once an American lady, after traveling through Japan, rightly remarked that Japanese talk like ventriloquists. Their movement of mouth and lips in talking is so little as to escape notice. They talk with nearly closed mouth so that during inspiration, a peculiar hissing sound is heard.

Americans and Europeans should, therefore regard Japanese vowels as a sort of unstressed or unaccented vowels uttered in more or less indifferent manner. Japanese on the other hand, when studying European languages, should particularly endeavor to pronounce all vowels in a much exaggerated manner in comparison to those of Japanese language.

The quality of Japanese vowels is summed up in the following:

i....somewhere between ee in eel and i in ill
e..somewhere between e in eight and e in egg
a....like a in art
o....somewhere between o in odd and o in oak
u..somewhere between u in put and u in rude

Variation in Japanese Vowels

The quality of Japanese vowels has not been the subject of study to any extent in Japan, as is shown by lack of books treating it. If one would pronounce a Japanese vowel in an improper manner, chances are that he would not be corrected or criticized by any teacher, except perhaps at the kindergarten stage. If two different shades of a Japanese vowel should be pronounced in succession, one would be at a loss to know or tell which is the correct sound and which wrong.

The quality of Japanese vowels given in the present chapter is the outcome of observation for many years. The average of sounds heard in middle Japan including Tokyo, Osaka and west is taken as a standard.

Vowels pronounced in north and extreme east are generally more close. Those of extreme west are more or less nasalized. Many elisions and contractions occur in Satsuma sounds.

As to the opening of lips and jaws, it also varies widely in different localities and various individuals. But the general variation in different districts of Japan is toward narrower if any. In loud speech, the general movement is much exaggerated and the lips and jaws naturally open wider.

Length of Japanese Vowels

Now we come to the most important facts about Japanese vowels, and that is the length of time consumed for a vowel. The length of vowels does not vary whether they are preceded by a consonant or not, as the consonantal modification affects the initial portion of a vowel without consuming any extra time.

Kindergarten children of Japan, soon after learning all the sounds contained in 'i-ro-ha', are able to pronounce all forty-seven sounds of kana in about twelve seconds. As the kana sounds are uttered at the uniform length, it follows that each kana syllable consumes about a quarter of a second. In ordinary conversation in Japanese, an individual kana sound would occupy time not far from this rate.

For the present, we will call a quarter of a second a unit of length of Japanese sounds. All sounds of kana are uttered in one unit. These we call short sounds. As kana, the elements of Japanese speech end in short vowel and the only final consonant being n, Japanese speech most often ends in short vowel or n. This is why conversation in Japanese often sounds to English ears to have abrupt ending. When English speech ends in a vowel, it is more frequently a long vowel.

There are other sounds which take exactly twice as long as the short, that is two units, and which is here called long sounds.

In English sounds, there is a certain amount of change in quality in short and long sounds of supposedly the same quality. For instance:

a in father (open), a in sofa (close)
i in machine (close), i in it (open)
u in rule (close), u in pull (open)
e in they (high), e in them (low)
o in old (close), o in obey (open)

Japanese vowels do not suffer in quality of sound when long or short, the long sound being simple prolongation of corresponding short sound. In case of Japanese long e, it tends to end somewhat like i, and long o tends to terminate in u quality, although in colloquial speech long e and o of uniform quality throughout are frequently heard. With long a, i and u, no appreciable change in quality, except perhaps a slight relaxation in the second half is noticeable. The rules of kana writing require a, i and u to be repeated to make them long, whereas long o is written ou and long e written ei. We find exact analogy in long o and a in English, especially that of British, that they assume u and i quality toward end.

Foreigners learning Japanese language usually overlook the fact that the long vowel should occupy exactly the time of two short vowels or two units.

In English, so called long vowels are not

always long in speech and short vowels, on the other hand, are often drawn out especially when emphasized. In French and German speeches there are long, medium and short vowels. But in Japanese language there are only two, namely long and short, and the long always take twice the time of the short. The short sound takes one unit and the long sound takes two units of time.

It is unfortunate that many Japanese proper names when written in Romaji are nearly always dispensed with signs or marks to show long vowels. This applies to cases of o and u. Other vowels present no difficulty, as e or i are followed by i for long sound, and a is very seldom prolonged.

Some of the more popular geographic and family names with long vowels with pronunciation and time-units are given below:

Written	Sounded	In Units
Kobe	Ko-o-be	3
Osaka	O-o-sa-ka	4
Kyoto	Kyo-o-to	3
Tokio	To-o-kyo-o	4
Nikko	Ni-k-ko-o	4
Kyushu	Kyu-u-shu-u	4
Hyogo	Hyo-o-go	3
Kofu	Ko-o-fu	3
Kyobashi	Kyo-o-ba-shi	4
Oshima	O-o-shi-ma	4
Omiya	O-o-mi-ya	4

Oiso	O-o-i-so	4
Oita	O-o-i-ta	4
Ito	I-to-o	3
Sato	Sa-to-o	3
Ota	O-o-ta	3
Kato	Ka-to-o	3
Naito	Na-i-to-o	4
Todo	To-o-do-o	4
Kwanto	Kwa-n-to-o	4
Soshu	So-o-shu-u	4
Taiko	Ta-i-ko-o	4
Shogun	Sho-o-gu-n	4
Judo	Ju-u-do-o	4

Originally all long vowels were marked with a dash or circumflex over them. But owing to the fact that such types are not available at times, the marks are often left out in print. Other devices for this purpose avoiding the use of special types are:

1. Doubling of a vowel to be sounded long.
2. Addition of i after e, and u or w after o.
3. Addition of h after a vowel to be prolonged.

But none of these as yet met the universal approval and came to general use.

Well established proper names with long vowels are not numerous. It is perhaps best not to alter the spelling of names already in general use. Fortunately they are not many enough to bar students from committing them to memory.

CHAPTER XI

JAPANESE CONSONANTS

Sounds of Japanese Consonants

Consonants used in Japanese speech are 14 in number . They are k, g, s, z, t, d, n, h, b, p, m, y, r and w. Each one of these are supposed to precede vowels a, i, u, e, o. But in Romaji method of spelling some discrepancies occur as has been already pointed out.

Among these consonants, the sound value of k, g, n, h, b, m and p are nearly equivalent to those of English, namely:

k—k in kind

g—g in go, never like g in gentle, even before e or i

n—n in no

h—h in he. For h before u, which is usually spelled fu—see below

b—be in bee

m—m in met, the humming stage or nasal hum with mouth closed just before opening the mouth for the vowel is very much shorter in comparison to that of English. The same applies to n, r, or s

p—p in pen.

For other consonants namely s, z, t, d, y, r, and w, the points of difference in sounds from those of English are explained below.

S is pronounced with position of tongue probably slightly behind to that of English, or more back portion of tongue is involved in production of Japanese s. Hence less hissing is heard.

Romaji spells kana of s line, as sa, shi, su, se, so. No Japanese are conscious that the second syllable is produced with a different consonant from the rest. Japanese s is phonetically the same before a or i. It is the foreign ears that mistook Japanese s before i to be sh in she, at early Meiji era. Older writings give si or ci for this sound.

The nature of the consonant does not vary throughout the line, but owing to the involvement of back portion of tongue and the indifferent manner in which all vowels are uttered, the sound for si (shi in Romaji) assumes the nature of sound intermediate between English see and she without rounding or puckering of lips.

The sound of z is the Japanese s vocalized. The majority of Japanese utter z with tongue briefly touching the roof of mouth. Then the sound produced will be more like ds or dz. There are others, however, who pronounce this consonant without contact of tongue to the roof of mouth, in which case the sound closely resembles that of z in zeal, the only difference being the back portion of tongue which is used.

T and D

In uttering the consonants t and d the Japanese seem to be slow in removing the tongue from the roof of mouth, especially when close vowels like i or u follows, resulting in sounds somewhat like chi, tsu, ji dzu.

The sounds of chi and ji should not be pronounced like chi in chick or ji in Jim, with usual puckering of lips. Japanese do not round lips for chi and ji.

Romaji spells t and d line of kana, thus:

ta chi tsu te to
da ji dzu de do

Apparently three different consonants are involved in each line, that is t, ch, ts and d, j, dz. Japanese usually are not conscious of this fact.

It is probable that the Japanese pronounce t or d lines with the idea of uttering kana of equal nature, but to foreign ears the five kana in a line sound as though made of three separate consonants through following reasons: (1) Japanese t and d are produced on area further back on the tongue and corresponding further back portion of palate than for English t and d; (2) slowness of removing the tongue from the position to that of the directly following vowel; (3) closeness or indifferent nature of Japanese vowels.

Relation of Z Line to D Line

In modern Japanese speech the second and third syllables of z and d lines are no more distinguishable in sounds, although different kana characters exist.

Modern Romaji spells these two lines thus:

za ji zu ze zo
da ji zu de do

There are reasons to believe ji, zu of z line differed from those of d line at former times; probably as zi, zu and ji, dsu. Japanese othography teaches and insists that the proper kana is used in a given word.

Y is Shorter and Weaker

Y before a, u and o is like y in English, although weaker and extremely short. Before e and i it is not sounded, kana characters for these positions lacking. One may find in Romaji ye is often spelled in place of e, especially for proper names, but the normal Japanese sound for such syllable is e.

W before a is not like w in wad. In English a after w is always broad because of highly rounded quality of English w. Japanese w is less ostentatious and is pronounced like a very short u. A short and slight approaching of lips precede a vowel so that it is heard only before a, and is not audible or entirely silent before other vowels. Special kana characters exist for wi, we and wo, although modern Japanese sounds for them are identical with i, e, and o.

H before a, i, e, o is sounded like that of English, but before u (which is written fu in Romaji), owing to the closeness of Japanese u, the approached lips cause this consonant to produce a frictional sound resembling f. But this sound is produced by the passage of breath through a narrow slit between lips, and is entirely different from English f, which is produced by air forcing through crevices created by light contact between upper teeth and lower lips.

JAPANESE R

Japanese r is a distinctive sound, having no parallel in European or in Chinese languages. Like other Japanese sounds there are varieties or Japanese r, but the usual and the most prevalent Japanese r is a tongue explosive, that is, the sound is produced like English d, with the difference that the tongue is made contact to the roof of mouth a little further behind, and is more relaxed, and the tip or front edge of the tongue only comes in a very light contact with the palate, the force of explosion being much weaker than for d.

Japanese r may be best understood if compared with some of r sounds in European languages.

1. Tongue trill voiced (French, German, Slavonians)
2. Tongue trill aspirate (Slavonic).
3. Tongue resistive voiced (Spanish)
4. Tongue resistive aspirate (Spanish)
5. Tongue moulded voiced (German, French)
6. Uvular trill voiced (German, French)
7. Uvular fricative voiced (German, French)
8. Tongue explosive voiced (Japanese).

Japanese r resembles t in forty, kitty in rapid colloquial utterance, when t is sounded somewhat like a very light d.

For Japanese r, therefore, tongue should be more relaxed than for d, and the touch of tongue to palate should be lighter and briefer than for d.

The fact that three hundred years ago when machine knitted goods were first imported to Japan by Portuguese and the word "medias" came to Japan, while the Japanese today call all machine knitted goods "meriyasu," proves the close relationship between Japanese r and European d.

Japanese Final N

The only final consonant n has a peculiar sound, different from English n or French liquid n. The English n is produced by voice escaping through the nose, with the mouth open but the front and side edges of tongue in contact with the roof of mouth behind the upper teeth completely shutting off the current of air from passing through the mouth. But for n before k or g the top of tongue at back position contacts the roof of mouth for shutting off the mouth passage, because the next coming sound k or g requires the extreme back part of tongue to be in contact with the roof of mouth.

The French final n is constructed in an entirely different manner. When n follows a vowel, it indicates that the vowel is nasalized: that is, the vowel sound is made with the nasal passage open. In other words, the sound of n is made at the same time with that of the vowel and not after it.

The Japanese final n is produced when the voice is emitted while both the nasal and oral passages are open, with the tongue and other mouth parts are at the state of complete relaxation and rest. If the mouth, tongue and the chin are at rest, a voice uttered will be neutral vowel, provided the passage to the nose is not open. The same sound with passage to the nose open is the Japanese final n.

It should be uttered in continuous breath but separately from the vowel preceding it, taking one unit of time for itself. If another vowel follows it, the Japanese final n should not impart any n quality to that vowel. This is made possible by the fact that in uttering the Japanese final n the tongue does not touch the roof of mouth.

Examples:

ten	te-n	in 2 units
sen-oh	se-n-o-o	in 4 units
ken-i	ke-n-i	in 3 units

Japanese final n is pronounced only when it precedes s, z, h, y or w, or when it ends a word. In other instances, variations from regular sound occur as follows:

1. Like ng in sing when before k or g.
2. Like English n when before ch, ts, t, d, n, r, all of which require contact of tongue with roof of mouth.
3. Like m before m, p, b, all of which require closing of lips. (Original Hepburn system of Romaji spelt m in place of n in these cases.)

Examples illustrating these variations of Japanese final n:

1. tenki   2. sentoh, renraku,   3. sanmyaku,
   jinguh   dendoh, enchaku,   sanpu,
               sentsuh, sennen.   kenbi.

Contracted or Doubled Consonants

These are usually results of combination of two or more characters, which if sounded separately would make un-euphonic connection. The sounds of k, s, t, sh, ch, ts and p

may be doubled, in which case they are spelled in Romaji as kk, ss, tt, ssh, tch and pp.

Examples: sekken, sessei, zattoh, sesshoh,
hatchaku, settsu, happi.

If the words in these examples were divided into sound units, they will be,

In Sound Units	Contraction of
se-k-ke-n	seki-ken
se-s-se-i	setsu-sei
za-t-to-h	zatsu-toh
se-s-sho-h	setsu-shoh
ha-t-cha-ku	hatsu-chaku
se-t-tsu	setsu-tsu
ha-p-pi	hatsu-hi

In pronouncing these, the compression
stage of k, t (of the third example) and p
is prolonged to occupy one extra unit. For
t in the fifth example, compression for Japanese ch, and for t in the sixth example, compression for ts are likewise to be prolonged
to occupy an extra unit of time. For s in
the second and fourth example, an English
s sound is to be uttered for the extra unit.
The rules for contracting or doubling consonants may be stated as follows:

In compounds of two or more Kanji, if
one ends with any one of ki, ku, chi or tsu
and the next begins with any one of k, t, h,
f, s or ch, in most cases the ending of the
first is omitted in pronunciation and the be-

ginning consonant of the second is doubled, except in case of h or f which is changed to p before doubling, and ch adds t before it instead of doubling.

Examples:

	If Pronounced Separately	Pronunciation In Compound
匹夫	(hiki-fu)	hippu
石火	(seki-ka)	sekka
學校	(gaku-koh)	gakkoh
獨步	(doku-ho)	doppo
一杯	(ichi-hai)	ippai
八方	(hachi-ho)	happoh
節儉	(setsu-ken)	sekken
必携	(hitsu-kei)	hikkei
卒倒	(sotsu-toh)	sottoh
屈曲	(kutsu-kyoku)	kukkyoku
決勝	(ketsu-shoh)	kesshoh
決着	(ketsu-chaku)	ketchaku

Doubling of m and n occurs in the same way, the sounds of which are like those of English, as given under the Japanese final n, but it is important to note that all doubled consonants take an extra unit of time in sounding.

In colloquial and provincial speech, the sounds of g, z, d, b are at times heard doubled. H, r, y and w are never occur doubled.

Combined Consonants

Other combinations of more than one consonant before a vowel are interposition of y or w between consonant and vowel. In other words, the consonants, k, g, s, z, ts, n, h, b, p, m, or r may precede ya, yu or yo. Likewise k or g may precede wa. These sounds are written in various ways by different systems of Romaji, as seen in European books on Oriental sounds by different authors. Some of them are shown below:

Kya, kia, kja, chia, quia; kyu, kiu, kju, chiu, quiu; kyo, kio, kjo, chio; gya, gia, ghia; gyu, giu, gju, ghiu; gyo, gio, gjo, ghio; sha, sya, sia, scha; shu, syu, sju, schu; sho, syo, sio, scho; ja, zya, zia, dsia, dzha; ju, zyu, zhu, dzhu; jo, zyo, zho, dsio, dsho; cha, tsya, tscha; chu, tsyu, tschu; cho, tsyo, tsio, tscho; nya, nia; nyu, niu; nyo, nio; hya, hia, hja; hyu, hiu; hyo, hio, hjo; bya, bia, bja; byu, biu; byo, bio, bjo; pya, pia; pyu, piu; pyo, pio; mya, miu; myu, miu; myo, mio; rya, ria; ryu, riu; ryo, rio; kwa, kua; gwa, gua.

Fortunately most of these variant spelling went out of use, except perhaps the proper names as Tokyo, Tokio; Kyoto, Kioto, etc. China is still in chaos in this respect, as more than a dozen authors still publish romanized Chinese in their own systems.

The pronunciation of combined consonants should be a simple matter when one understands the following directions. The consonants k, g, s, z, etc., are to be sounded as given in chapter on Japanese consonants and the rest of the syllable is to be pronounced as ya, yu, yo or wa as the case may be, being careful to combine the initial consonant to it intimately so that no extra time is consumed thereby.

Variation in Sounds

Since there are no rules of pronunciation or system of sound teaching ever incorporated in Japanese educational curriculum, owing partly to the extreme simplicity of Japanese vowels and consonants, and also to the fact that there exists a considerable distance between any two nearest Japanese vowels, resulting in a wide range to any one of vowels which is allowed. It is of natural sequence that a wide variety of quality of Japanese vowels and to some extent of consonants, may occur without arousing any notice by the native Japanese ears.

These variations may be categorically divided into four kinds, namely that which is due to time, to individual, to provinciality and to circumstances.

Variation According to Time

As has been pointed out elsewhere, there is no mode of exactly recording sounds of the Japanese language, it is extremely hard to study variation in Japanese sounds at different ages. But changes in sounds in time is the quality of any living language, there is no doubt that changes are occuring in sounds of the Japanese language.

From the fact that some documents of the 16th Century concerning Japan (preserved in Europe) contains names such as Nangasaki, Amanguchi, etc., it may be surmised that the nasalized g or ng sound must have been heard in western Japan at former times. For some recent changes, see Chapter XV on early Japanese sounds.

Individualism and Provincialism

Personal difference in wideness, narrowness, highness, lowness, openness and closeness, etc., of vowels constitutes the individualism. Variations in consonant qualities, semi-vocalized aspects and sibilants occur in different localities, too numerous to mention.

Some of the conspicous ones are nasalized g in not initial syllables heard in Kwanto region; tongue trill r of Yedo people; doubling of vocalized explosives in Satsuma speech; f like character of h sound in Izumo, Hoki, etc.; closeness of all vowels in northern Japan; distinct w sound before i, e, o, in Kyuhshuh, Toyama, Niigata, etc.

Circumstantial Variations

Foreigners learning Japanese, or foreign born children of Japanese, who are fast increasing in number usually learn elements of non-Japanese language prior to that of Japanese; put foreign influence to Japanese consonants. Their sounds of Japanese f, j, y, w, r, ch, sh, etc., are patterned to some European sounds (mostly English). When learning Japanese they do not appreciate the slight but fundamental difference in construction of the Japanese consonants named. The results are, these people almost invariably pronounce

f with distinct teeth-lip friction instead of a soft blow between lips.

j with distinctly puckered lips.

y so distinctly that it may be heard even before e or i.

w so strong with rounding of lips as to be heard before i, u, e, o.

r from tongue molded variety of English to uvular frictive of French-German.

ch with distinctly puckered lips instead of indifferent position of lips.

sh with distinctly puckered lips instead of indifferent position.

CHAPTER XII

ROMAJI

Thus far we have considered the true Japanese sounds in reference to English sounds. Now we are in position to consider the Romaji, the foreign style of writing Japanese languarge.

The history of Romaji dates back to the 16th Century, when Francis Xavier came to Japan to preach Christian doctrine. Dutch and Portuguese merchants also frequented Japanese shores for the purpose of trade in those days. Some books have been published in the Japanese language written in European characters.

The modern Romaji owes its origin to Rev. Dr. J. C. Hepburn, who practiced medicine along side of him missionary work in Japan during early years of Meipi. He wrote a Japanese-English dictionary, in which romanized Japanese were used, and published it in or about the year 1872 A. D. He is probably among the first to teach Japanese how to write Romaji. Keio Gijuku, founded by Yukichi Fukuzawa also published shortly after a guide for writing romanized Japanese.

Romaji is the name given to all systems

of writing the Japanese language with con-
sonants with English sounds. Romaji of
Hepburn type is the kind introduced by Dr.
Hepburn, in his dictionary.

The name "Romaji" itself is probably of
his own creation. Although various other
systems have been created and advocated,
some taking pattern to English, others German, French, etc., none of them had enough
followers to make the new system para-
mount over Hepburns. Some went to sug-
gest Capitalization of nouns as in German.
Others suggested new rules on division of
words and punctuation, etc. But the most
widely accepted Hepburns system still remains, though some modifications were in-
evitable.

The following is the modern Romaji generally used, nearly corresponding to the original Hepburn.

a	i	u	e	o
ka	ki	ku	ke	ko
sa	shi	su	se	so
ta	chi	tsu	te	to
na	ni	nu	ne	no
ha	hi	fu	he	ho
ma	mi	mu	me	mo
ya		yu		yo
ra	ri	ru	re	ro
wa				
n				

ga	gi	gu	ge	go
za	ji	zu	ze	zo
da			de	do
ba	bi	bu	be	bo
pa	pi	pu	pe	po

kya	kyu	kyo
sha	shu	sho
cha	chu	cho
nya	nyu	nyo
hya	hyu	hyo
mya	myu	myo
rya	ryu	ryo
gya	gyu	gyo
ja	ju	jo
bya	byu	byu
pya	pyu	pyo

These hundred syllables and one final n are all that is necessary in writing Japanese, except the occasional doubling of consonants. Consonants which can be doubled are k, s, t, n, m, and p. Other consonants h, y, r, w, g, z, j, d, and be are never doubled. When necessary to double the consonantal sound ch, the spelling tch is used. Likewise ssh is used for doubling of sh.

The length of vowels in Romaji is modified or prolonged by addition of a dash or circumflex over such vowels. In this work as well as in author's "Dictionary of Japanese Characters," h after a vowel is substituted for a dash or a circumflex over it, to serve the purpose of showing that such vowel is to be sounded twice as long.

Heretofore it was common to omit the dash or circumflex over vowels whenever such a type in print is not available. It may be suggested here, that the h after any vowel be regarded as equivalent and interchangeable with a dash or circumflex over the vowel, much in the same fashion as Germans use e after a or o and consider it to be equivalent and interchangeable with an "Umlaut" mark or two dots over such vowels. In this case, if a vowel comes after such h in the same word, a hyphen between the h and the vowel will prevent the error of attaching the h to the vowel.

Romanized Kana

The number of Romaji syllables is 101, but the number of kana characters is 73 including 25 modified kana. These discrepancies can be explained by the fact, that Romaji represents Japanese sounds and the kana is a set of written characters. It is obvious that in referring to kana characters, Romaji cannot be readily used. Hence the necessity of improvising the Romanized kana or alphabetical representation of written kana. They are:

a	i	u	e	o
ka	ki	ku	ke	ko
sa	si	su	se	so
ta	ti	tu	te	to
na	ni	nu	ne	no
ha	hi	hu	he	ho
ma	mi	mu	me	mo
ya		yu		yo
ra	ri	ru	re	ro
wa	wi		we	wo
n				

ga	gi	gu	ge	go
za	zi	zu	ze	zo
da	di	du	de	do
ba	bi	bu	be	bo
pa	pi	pu	pe	po

Among the above, wi, we, wo, di, du are pronounced like i, e, o, zi, zu respectively in modern Japanese pronounciation, making sixty-eight different sounds in all. Sometimes h is sounded like w and y is silent. The readers are referred to Japanese orthography (chapter xiv) for further details of these sound changes.

Japanese System of Romaji

Among many different systems of Romaji rendering of Japanese language, there is one which is called the Japanese system, which although is nearly as old in its history as the ordinary type, did not occupy a prominent place until recently, when its advocators are nearly successful in making various official bodies connected with ministries of army, navy, education, and communication adopt this system officially.

Characters of this system are identical with the romanized kana given in the fore-going section. Although one who is familiar with the ordinary or Hepburn system of romaji can easily read the Japanese system, as the alterations are limited to only a few characters, the real difference is fundamental. The Hepburn system is based on the sounds heard, while the Japanese system is based on written kana, except in compounds. As far as individual kana characters are concerned the latter system is an excellent one to perpetuate Japanese orthography.

As will be pointed out later in the chapter on Japanese orthography, the trouble in correct use of kana lies in the absence of eye training; the Japanese system will be able to solve this problem by constantly presenting before the eyes the correct kana spelling. But the Japanese system goes only half way in solving the problem of orthography, as it uses compounds nearly equal to those of Hepburn system. If it were aimed to reveal all the secrets of correct use of kana, the Japanese system should have pursued the policy of separating compounds into their component parts, for instance: Choh (meaning long) as ti-a-u; choh (heavy) as ti-yo-u; choh (morning) as te-u; choh (butterfly) as te-hu; etc.

Japanese orthography would sooner or later pass into historical oblivion. Still it would be a hard thing to throw off what we are used to have all at once. The Japanese system would be the most appropriate thing, for the present, to be used for romanizing the Japanese language, as it teaches to a certain extent the secret of Japanese orthography.

Because of the fact that those who know Hepburn system of Romaji can easily read any writing in Japanese system of Romaji and vice versa, we do not see any reason why advocators on either side should oppose each other so, pointing out defects of the other system and urging the general adoption of their own. They might as well cooperate in making the nation understand the importance of throwing off the yoke of Kanji and taking up the simpler system, such as kana or Romaji of either Japanese Hepburn system. Even kana system, if division of words were made in the same manner as that of Romaji would certainly make a great improvement over Kanji.

Considering the difference or distance between kanji on one hand and kana or Romaji of any system on the other, the difference
in construction of kana and Romaji is so in-
significantly small, that the adherents of
kana and Romaji systems should find no difficulties in cooperation toward their common
object of throwing kanji off the sphere of
Japanese language.

The most important point which needs em-
phasis is that kana or Romaji spelling of
words should be brought before the eyes
frequently enough to make them as familiar
as kanji of today; and only then the real
merits of kana or Romaji over kanji may be
made manifest.

Efforts necessary to learn all these systems namely kana, Romaji of Hepburn type
and that of Japanese system would be insig-
nificant if compared to that needed to learn
kanji. If advocators of these systems would
hold a conference and study the best methods of division of words, punctuation, capitalization, adoption of omission of certain
words etc., and would unite their efforts toward driving kanji out of popular use, instead of finding each other's faults, and
teach all three systems simultaneously, they
would certainly be rewarded with much
earlier success. As to the comparative merits
of the three systems, time would be the sole
judge. In course of a few years of actual
use, the best of the three will survive the

rest, or else each would find its respective place of adaptability and usefulness; for example, kana and Hepburn system in literature and science, and the Japanese system in commercial world.

Kanji may be reserved for higher grade of learning in the same line as Sanskrit, Hebrew, Greek or Latin today are studied in high schools and colleges.

The syllables of Japanese system of Romaji are almost the same as Romanized kana given on page 84, in addition to which following syllables are used for combined sounds.

kya	kyu	kyo
sya	syu	syo
tya	tyu	tyo
nya	nyu	nyo
hya	hyu	hyo
mya	myu	myo
rya	ryu	ryo
gya	gyu	gyo
zya	zyu	zyo
dya	dyu	dyo
bya	byu	byo
pya	pyu	pyo

CHAPTER XIII

ACCENTS AND STRESSES

Speech in any language is not a monotonous succession of words. A part of a certain word, the whole word or a group of words is uttered more forcibly than others, that is, accented or stressed.

For the sake of clearness in explanation the word "stress" is here meant to represent the more forcible utterance of a word or a group of words, and the word "accent" to represent the more forcible utterance of a syllable in a word.

In most of European languages including English, French, German, Spanish, etc., the stress is laid on a word or words, where the meaning is to be brought more conspicuously. Take an example in English:

The **book** is on the table.—The book (not the magazine).

The book **is** on the table.—It is there, now.

The book is **on** the table.—On, not below the table.

The book is on the **table.**—On the table, not on the desk.

Here the words in bold types are pronounced fully in louder tone and at higher pitch, usually more slowly.

In the same manner, in other European languages, as well as in Japanese language, the stress on words is laid to bring out the meaning above others.

It seems that the use of stress on important words in speech is universal in any language, and the Japanese is no exception to the rule. Therefore no further comment is necessary.

Accents on Syllables

When one pronounces a syllable more forcibly than others, the pitch of voice is raised slightly. This is of natural consequence, as when more force is used in utterance, more air tends to escape, the vocal cords are involuntarily narrowed in their unconscious efforts to prevent too rapid escape of air. The result is the raising of pitch, accompanied by more force and loudness.

The accent is the raising of pitch and force, so that the syllable accented stands out over others. Accents in some language are more in pitch than the force, while in others it is opposite.

The general pitch of voice of one person is different from that of another person, when the size of the larynx and vocal cords differs or the distance of vocal cords from the mouth varies or when both of these variations occur together. This is why the voice of women is higher than that of men, or the voice of children is higher than that of adults. This general or natural pitch of voice has nothing to do with accents.

The accent is the raising of pitch and force on a particular syllable above the level of adjacent syllables so that the syllable accented stands out over others.

Accents in European Languages

Various consonants or vowels of English language for instance, have natural pitch of different levels. The more closed the air passage, the sound is sharper. The natural pitch of consonants beginning from the highest will be in the order of s, ts, th, f, sh (ch), t, k, p, and of vowels i, e, u, o, a (in short sounds). But these natural or inherent pitches of vowels or consonants are not considered in this work.

In English or German languages, accents on syllables are given in dictionaries. In French, there exists a general rule to accentuate the last full vowel of a word. In Spanish all vowels to be accented are so marked. Places of accents seem to be peculiar to each language. It is found that the words of same Latin or Greek root, finding places in English, German, French or Spanish languages do not have accents on same syllables thus:

English	German
com′rade	ka-me-rad′
phot′o-graph	pho-to-graph′
o′ver-come	ue-ber-kom′men

English	French
lect'ure	lec-ture'
mo'ment	mo-ment'
in'fant	en-fant'

English	Spanish
en-coun'ter	en-con-trar'
man'ner	ma-ne'ra

French	Spanish
coe'ur	co-ra-zon'
e'sto-mac	e-sto'ma-go

Importance of Accents

Each word in most European languages has a definite accent; whereas in Japanese language the situation is entirely different. There is no definite accent on any of the syllables of a Japanese word. No mention is ever made of the accent in any of Japanese books, nor does any of the books in English for the instruction of Japanese language give any light on the subject.

A successful acquirement of any foreign language lies in getting correct accents on syllables and right stress on words as the natives are accustomed to do. The Japanese language lacks entirely in guide to accentuation. It is left to the discretion of a speaker. Hence it often varies according to the individual or locality. It may also have changed with the time. It again varies according to the situation of a word in a sentence.

Therefore no hard and fast rules as to accentuation in Japanese words are possible. Still there is a general usage to accent a certain syllable of a word. If a majority of educated Japanese people give accent to a certain syllable in a given word, it may be given to posterity as a record of what is heard at the present age, at the same time to serve as a guide for learners from outside, including thousands of foreign-born children of Japanes parentage, whose tendencies are to create a new departure from correct Japanese speech, and who are already forming a sort of foreignized Japanese.

It becomes necessary to mark Japanese accents, which are different from those of English or other European languages in many ways, and therefore require a new method.

Peculiarity of Japanese Accents

Following are the points of difference of Japanese accents from European accents:

1. Two or more syllables may take accents in succession.

2. Long vowels are composed of two time units. Each unit may take an accent independent of the other.

3. Final n or isolated consonants, as the first element of doubled consonant, may take an accent.

The first step in marking accents is to divide words into syllables.

Since there is no precedent in syllablization of Japanese words, an arbitrary division of words into the time units is resorted to, and the following simple rules thereto are made.

Rules of syllablization of Japanese words:

1. All short vowels make one syllable.
2. All long vowels make two syllables.
3. All consonantal sounds preceding a vowel are attached to the vowel without additional syllable.
4. Final n forms a separate syllable.
5. First element of doubled consonants form a separate syllable.

Examples for above, if the syllables are divided with hyphens

1.   a-o-i, e-i-se-i
2.   o-h,ki-i, tsu-h-ko-h
3.   ka-sa-ne-ru, cha-ku-ji-tsu
4.   sen-n-ke-n, shi-m-bu-n
5.   ga-k-ko-h, ze-t-ta-i-te-ki.

Majority of educated Japanese today would pronounce words of above examples in the manner described below:

Accent on the second syllable for a-o-i, cha-ku-ji-tsu.

Accents on the second, third and fourth syllables for e-i-se-i, tsu-u-ko-h, ka-sa-ne-ru, se-n-ke-n, shi-m-bu-n, ga-k-koh.

Accents on the second and third syllables for o-h-ki-i.

Accents on all syllables except the first for ze-t-ta-i-te-ki.

It is obvious that the usual accent mark ′ would not answer the purpose of indicating more than one syllable in succession pronounced with higher pitch than the rest.

The first attempt in giving accents to Japanese words has been therefore made by the author in his dictionary of Japanese characters published in 1928, in which hyphens of higher and lower levels were used to represent higher and lower pitches of tone. A few examples taken from that dictionary are here given merely to show how effective they are in giving time units or syllables and those which are to be accented or pronounced in higher pitch.

Kohgyoh (‐‑‑‑); yuhwaku (‐‑‑‑); tsutomu (‐‑‑); renmen (‐‑‑‑); teikoku (‐‑‑‑); dohri (‐‑‑); kenri (‐‑‑); akiraka (‐‑‑‑).

For other examples, the readers are referred to the Dictionary of Japanese Characters, which gives similar kind of accents to more than 7000 Japanese words.

By the way, this new method of marking accents with short horizontal bars, will be handy to indicate the more minute details of English accents. The author uses this system in noting the pitch changes within a syllable of short words, as heard in colloquial English, thus: yes? (--), yes! (--), no? (--), no! (--), huh? (--), huh? (--), oh (--), oh (--), old (----), etc.

Elision of Vowels

In quick speech, certain unaccented vowels become so weak that the voice is suppressed and the breathing alone remains. It does not however mean that the vowel is omitted altogether. It is uttered without voice or vibration of vocal cord, similar to a whisper. This peculiarity is confined to an unaccented vowel after aspirate consonants. Some former writers expressed this kind of elision of sound by an apostrophe. Thus:

H'to (hito), h'tots' (hitotsu), arimash'ta (arimashita), chak'chak' (chakuchaku), teikok' (teikoku), arimas' (arimasu).

CHAPTER XIV

JAPANESE ORTHOGRAPHY

As has been mentioned in the chapter of kana, there are 48 characters of kana and 25 modifications thereof by addition of dots or circles. Among these, there are five pairs of homophonous kana, besides the five which have dual sounds. This makes the number of different sounds which may be written with kana 68. Use is also made of two kinds of repeating signs and one prolonging sign but these have no relation to sounds of kana.

There are 101 single sounds in spoken Japanese, which may be written in Romaji. Kana is quite inadequate to write all these sounds. Recourse is therefore made to substitutes of two or three kana characters combined. As there is no special signs for combining, kana characters are written one after another, so that they could be read either combined or separately.

In some cases, several different combinations are possible for one sound. These facts together with the presence of five homophonous pairs of kana and five kana with dual sounds, necessitate rules for correct use of kana of "kanazukai" or Japanese orthography.

"Kanazukai" is divided into two sections, namely: that which applies to sounds of of characters and the other which treats of correct use of kana in writing Japanese language proper. These are called "Jion Kanazukai" and "Kokugo Kanazukai" respectively.

There are proper books of instruction for correct use of kana. The students are referred to one of Japanese grammars. In this work, which does not aim to give instructions in this direction, are given a few examples, merely for the purpose of showing that Japanese students are required to learn to write for a given word one particular kana and not another although of same sound.

In the following table "Jion" and "Kokugo" orthography are given mixed. The first column gives characters or words. The second column the correct kana, the third column, Romanized kana, the fourth column the sounds in Romaji.

Characters or Words	Correct Kana	Romanized Kana	Actual Sounds
意	い	i	i
井	ゐ	wi	i
舞	(ま)ひ	hi	i
乙	いつ	i-tu	itsu
聿	ゐつ	wi-tu	itsu

Characters or Words	Correct Kana	Romanized Kana	Actual Sounds
生	いき	i ki	iki
域	ゐき	wi ki	iki
因	いん	i n	in
員	ゐん	wi n	in
江	え	e	e
繪	ゑ	we	e
上	(う)へ	he	e
永	えい	e i	ei
衛	ゑい	we i	ei
閲	えつ	e-tu	etsu
越	ゑつ	we-tu	etsu
延	えん	e n	en
圓	ゑん	we n	en
御	お	o	o
尾	を	wo	o
顔	(か)ほ	ho	o
央	あう	a u	oh
押	あふ	a hu	oh
應	おう	o u	oh
翁	をう	wo u	oh
王	わう	wa u	oh

Characters or Words	Correct Kana	Romanized Kana	Actual Sounds
億	おく	o ku	oku
屋	をく	wo ku	oku
乙	おつ	o-tu	otsu
越	をつ	wo-tu	otsu
音	おん	o n	on
溫	をん	wo n	on
加	か	ka	ka
花	くわ	ku wa	ka
江	かう	ka u	koh
甲	かふ	ka hu	koh
劫	こふ	ko hu	koh
厚	こう	ko u	koh
皇	くわう	ku wa u	koh
開	かい	ka-i	kai
會	くわい	ku-wa-i	kai
各	かく	ka-ku	kaku
畫	くわく	ku-wa-ku	kaku
渴	かつ	ka-tu	katsu
活	くわつ	ku-wa- tu	katsu
甘	かん	ka-n	kan
完	くわん	ku-wa-n	kan

Characters or Words	Correct Kana	Romanized Kana	Actual Sounds
京	きやう	ki-ya-u	kyoh
共	きよう	ki-yo-u	kyoh
教	けう	ke-u	kyoh
協	けふ	ke-hu	kyoh
球	きう	ki-u	kyuh
急	きふ	ki-hu	kyuh
宮	きゆう	ki-yu-u	kyuh
雅	が	ga	ga
畫	ぐわ	gu-wa	ga
害	がい	ga-i	gai
外	ぐわい	gu-wa-i	gai
雁	がん	ga-n	gan
丸	ぐわん	gu-wa-n	gan
行	ぎやう	gi-ya-u	gyoh
凝	ぎよう	gi-yo-u	gyoh
堯	げう	ge-u	gyoh
業	げふ	ge-hu	gyoh
艘	さう	sa-u	soh
挿	さふ	sa-hu	soh
宗	そう	so-u	soh

Characters or Words	Correct Kana	Romanized Kana	Actual Sounds
省	しやう	si-ya-u	shoh
昇	しょう	si-yo-u	shoh
小	せう	se-u	shoh
妾	せふ	se-hu	shoh
州	しう	si-u	shuh
智	しふ	si-hu	shuh
衆	しゆう	si-yu-u	shuh
邪	じや	zi-ya	ja
搦	ぢや(く)	di-ya	ja
若	じやく	zi-ya-ku	jaku
雀	ぢやく	di-ya-ku	jaku
字	じ	zi	ji
治	ぢ	di	ji
食	じき	zi-ki	jiki
直	ぢき	di-ki	jïki
字句	じく	zi-ku	jiku
軸	ぢく	di-ku	jiku
實	じつ	zi-tu	jitsu
秩	ぢつ	di-tu	jitsu
仁	じん	zi-n	jin
陣	ぢん	di-n	jin

Characters or Words	Correct Kana	Romanized Kana	Actual Sounds
受	じゆ	zi-yu	ju
住	ぢゆ(う)	di-yu	ju
述	じゆつ	zi-yu-tu	jutsu
朮	ぢゆつ	di-yu-tu	jutsu
助	じょ	zi-yo	jo
女	ぢょ	di-yo	jo
上	じやう	zi-ya-u	joh
乘	じょう	zi-yo-u	joh
饒	ぜう	ze-u	joh
接	ぜふ	ze-hu	joh
杖	ぢやう	di-ya-u	joh
濃	ぢょう	di-yo-u	joh
條	でう	de-u	joh
帖	でふ	de-hu	joh
辱	じよく	zi-yo-ku	joku
濁	ぢよく	di-yo-ku	joku
柔	じう	zi-u	juh
十	じふ	zi-hu	juh
從	じゆう	zi-yu-u	juh
住	ぢゆう	di-yu-u	juh

Characters or Words	Correct Kana	Romanized Kana	Actual Sounds
手	ず	zu	zu
圖	づ	du	zu
蕊	ずゐ	zu-wi	zui
頭位	づゐ	du-wi	zui
造	ざう	za-u	zoh
雜	ざふ	za-hu	zoh
增	ぞう	zo-u	zoh
橙	たう	ta-u	toh
答	たふ	to hu	toh
豆	とう	to-u	toh
長	ちやう	ti-ya-u	choh
重	ちょう	ti-yo-u	choh
朝	てう	te-u	choh
蝶	てふ	te-hu	choh
宙	ちう	ti-u	chuh
蟄	ちふ	ti-hu	chuh
中	ちゆう	ti-yu-u	chuh
袋	なう	na-u	noh
納	なふ	na-hu	noh
農	のう	no-u	noh

Characters or Words	Correct Kana	Romanized Kana	Actual Sounds
女	にょう	ni-yo-u	nyoh
捻	ねふ	ne-hu	nyoh
繞	ねう	ne-u	nyoh
柔	にう	ni-u	nyuh
入	にふ	ni-hu	nyuh
乳	にゆう	ni-yu-u	nyuh
方	はう	ha-u	hoh
法	はふ	ha-hu	hoh
奉	ほう	ho-u	hoh
法	ほふ	ho-hu	hoh
表	へう	he-u	hyoh
兵	ひやう	hi-ya-u	hyoh
氷	ひよう	hi-yo-u	hyoh
茅	ばう	ba-u	boh
剖	ぼう	bo-u	boh
乏	ばふ	ba-hu	boh
乏	ぼふ	bo-hu	boh
猫	べう	be-u	byoh
病	びやう	bi-ya-u	byoh
毛	まう	ma-u	moh
蒙	もう	mo-u	moh
明	みやう	mi-ya-u	myoh
妙	めう	me-u	myoh

Characters or Words	Correct Kana	Romanized Kana	Actual Sounds
植	(う)う	u	yu
云	(い)ふ	hu	yu
生	(は)ゆ	yu	yu
尤	いう	i-u	yuh
勇	ゆう	yu-u	yuh
邑	いふ	i-hu	yuh
夕	ゆふ	yu-hu	yuh
用	よう	yo-u	yoh
羊	やう	ya-u	yoh
妖	えう	e-u	yoh
葉	えふ	e-hu	yoh
老	らう	ra-u	roh
蠟	らふ	ra-hu	roh
弄	ろう	ro-u	roh
良	りやう	ri-ya-u	ryoh
稜	りよう	ri-yo-u	ryoh
料	れう	re-u	ryoh
獵	れふ	re-hu	ryoh
流	りう	ri-u	ryuh
粒	りふ	ri-hu	ryuh
龍	りゆう	ri-yu-u	ryuh
河	(か)は	ha	wa
泡	(あ)わ	wa	wa

Difficulties of Japanese Orthography

In English language, spelling lessons occupy a large portion of primary school language lessons. The knowledge acquired from these lessons is strengthened as pupils advance, as the correct examples present themselves in daily reading of books, magazines or newspapers.

The situation in Japanese orthography is quite different from that of English. It is true that in primary schools, Japanese children are taught correct use of kana, but it covers rudiments only in most cases. As they advance, however, the Kanji or ideographic script occupies most of the pupil's time. The more they advance, the more they learn difficult Kanji and see less of kana. The difficulties of Japanese orthography lie in lack of eye training, which for example in English language automatically fortifies the spelling knowledge acquired in primary schools.

Hence the rules of Japanese orthography remains always difficult, and it is the domain of the very learned men only.

Movements to remedy the difficulty of Japanese orthography appeared from time to time during last fifty years. Some of these movements were made by committee appointed by the Department of Education. Various forms and simplification of "kana-

zukai" or the use of kana have been suggested. Men who are more or less in higher
level of Japanese education opposed these
new departures.

The latest suggestion by the committee
for the investigation of Japanese language
appointed by the Minister of Education gives
what is called "Hatsuon-shiki-Kanazukai" or
phonetic orthography, in which all difficulties of Japanese orthography are entirely
removed. But it is a question whether this
new system will ever meet the general approval.

In transcribing foreign words or names
in kana, it is the modern usage to use a dash
after any kana, to serve the purpose of prolonging the sound of the kana. The dash
may be used vertically or horizontally as
the case may require. Thus:

ロ　ア　レ　　ロ ー
｜　｜　｜　　
ト　ス　　　ア ー ト

レ ー ス

It seems that the practice of using a dash
mixed with kana in transcribing foreign
sounds as illustrated above met the general
sanction, perhaps through lack of better
method.

If the insistence of kana adherents would
have its way and the days will come when
the kana writing replaces kanji altogether,

the orthographically correct kana spelling would be universally learned in a short time. Then the difficulties of Japanese orthography would be entirely dispelled and forgotten, as they are nothing if compared to the spelling in English language.   All one would have to do is to memorize a couple of hundred kana combinations while in English it would amount to many thousands.

To illustrate the above points: if English language would adopt certain characters or signs for words like girl, school, high, low, pleasure, belief, many etc., and these spelling were very seldom seen in print or writing for a period of several centuries; the difficulty of English orthography no doubt would be more than ten fold that of Japanese orthography.

CHAPTER XV

EARLY JAPANESE SOUNDS

We have no adequate records of Japanese sounds which had been in use centuries ago. But from the fact that the rules of orthography insists use of one particular kana and not another in a given word, or one particular combination of kana and not another for a given word, we can surmise that the sounds have not been for all ages the same in these instances.

Variety in ways of writing makes us presume the corresponding variety in sounds which at some former times had existed. One minor change, quite fittingly illustrating this point has actually occurred in the last fifty years.

The sounds kwa and gwa were distinguished from ka and ga in sounds as well as in writing, during the early years of Meiji. Today, the distinction is observed in writing only. The popular sounds are the same now in both cases, that is kwa and gwa are pronounced like ka and ga.

The following table illustrates them.

Characters	Kana	Sounds 50 Years Ago	Sounds At Present
加下可歌 家香價夏 }	か	ka	ka
火化花果 瓜科貨過 }	‥くわ	kwa	ka
牙雅我 ‥‥‥‥	が	ga	ga
瓦臥畫 ‥‥‥	ぐわ	gwa	ga
介改開解‥‥‥	かい	kai	kai
會回灰快‥‥‥	くわい	kwai	kai
害慨‥‥‥‥‥	がい	gai	gai
外‥‥‥‥‥‥	ぐわい	gwai	gai
各革‥‥‥‥‥	かく	kaku	kaku
畫獲‥‥‥‥‥	くわく	kwaku	kaku
割渴‥‥‥ ‥	かつ	katsu	katsu
活滑 ‥‥‥‥	くわつ	kwatsu	katsu
合‥‥‥‥ ‥	がつ	gatsu	gatsu
月‥‥‥‥‥‥	ぐわつ	gwatsu	gatsu
寒甘間感‥‥‥	かん	kan	kan
完官卷患‥‥‥	くわん	kwan	kan
眼雁‥‥‥‥‥	がん	gan	gan
丸願‥‥‥‥‥	ぐわん	gwan	gan

So the difference in sounds of fifty years ago, in above given instances became lost and now the rules of orthography alone remain. If all other rules of Japanese orthography were remains of originally differentiated sounds, as some authorities assert, then it may be said that the Japanese sounds have tendencies of becoming simplified.

One kanji having present pronunciation of **oh** and requiring to be **wa-u** if written in kana, has been until recently universally used for **wa** sound, and that is 王

This fortifies the opinion that the diversity in kana writing means the corresponding diversity in sounds formerly.

The reason why Japanese sounds tend to drift toward the simplest inspite of the rules of orthography is quite obvious. Japanese have no phonetics or science of speech sounds. The mode of producing sounds or pronunciation is left entirely to the natural course it may take. Among illiterates, such sounds with slight phonetic difference as **shin, shun; chin, chun; jin, jun;** are already becoming confused in actual speech.

If it keeps on going at this rate, all syllables ending in **un** may become confused with that ending in **in,** so that at some future time, the difference in sounds between **un** and **in** may be historical and not actual, as are the rules of Japanese orthography today, who knows?

Influence of Romaji on Sounds

Popular Romaji spelling of **jujitsu, Shinyo Maru,** etc., are not correct Japanese sounds. They should be spelled **juhjutsu, Shun-yoh Maru,** if correct sounds of today are written. These examples show that the Romaji spelling may influence change of Japanese sounds.

Japanese children born in America can utter sounds as **yi, ye, wi, we, wu, wo,** with no difficulty. They pronounce **ye** in such names as Inouye, Uyeda, etc., as easy as **ye** in yes. Likewise, f in such words as furui, fukai, etc., is pronounced with regular teeth-lip f, instead of regular Japanese f with lips approached. Under the same category come also j, sh, ch, r, etc.

Germans say Yapan when written Japan. Some Europeans pronounce Jokohama for Yokohama, Jeddo for Yedo (Japanese pronunciation is Edo). Capital I and J are identical in German. Phonetically J and Y are nearly the same, the difference being chiefly in the force of utterance.

Thus it will be seen that the Romaji to some measure contributes to the alteration of Japanese sounds.

General Remarks

During the last 1500 years of time, Japanese sounds are seen to be undergoing "phonetic decay" of Max Müller. We took in from China over five hundred different sounds and now we have a little over three hundred. Even during last half century, we are in process of losing still more sounds.

On the other hand, new terms coined after Meiji restoration to keep pace with world progress, together with imported and popularized foreign words added to the Japanese vocabulary, are so numerous that they occupy fully ninety per cent of all Japanese words in daily papers. It may be said that the process of dialectical regeneration is now in full swing.

Of course at former times also, new Japanese compounds had been created from time to time according to the needs of the age, as are seen in older Japanese literature. But at no time, it is believed, the coining of new terms and adaptation and incorporation of foreign words into Japanese vocabulary had been performed so much as during the last fifty years.

Although announced as a book on Phonetics of Japanese Language, the real phonetics is covered in only two chapters in this work, and other dozen or more chapters are devoted to Japanese writing. This was a necessity, because any Japanese sound, in order to explain its sound value, must be represented by one of the three different methods of writing, namely kanji which are characters imported from China, Japanese kana which are derived from kanji, or Romaji which is Japanese language rendered in English characters. Relations between kanji, kana and Romaji are so complicated that, in order to make it clear to beginners, it had to take so many chapters of non-phonetic matter. Yet it will be of value to beginners in Japanese language, as they may be helped to learn many facts relating to those three forms of writing.

ERRATA

It is unfortunate that in spite of utmost care which has been exercised during type-setting and printing the following few errors have been found.

Page	Line	Wrong	Correct
17	14	sound	form
23	16	maru	masu
33	1	to read kana	to read by kana
35	15	grawichoh	gwaichoh
37	2	fu hiao,	fu hiao che,
40	5	尺圉	尺噩
58	3	teuse	tense
71	8	(German, French)	(English, German)
80	19	Meipi	Meiji
81	12	Capitalization	capitalization
86	30	Japanese	Japanese or

GLOSSARY

Accent—Accent on a syllable. The accent on a word is designated by stress in this work.

Chinese Character—Character or word sign consisting of one or more strokes limited with a square space, originated and used in Chinese language. Japan is also using Chinese characters during last 1500 years.

Chinese Ideographic Script—Same as Chinese character.

Chinese Sounds—Sounds of Chinese characters as given in China. Also sounds of Chinese characters as taught in Japan. The latter often differ from those heard in China, and yet they are known as Chinese sounds because they are taught first by Chinese.

Chosenese Alphabet—A phonetic alphabet of Korea.

Classical Chinese—Pure Chinese composition consisting of Chinese characters only. Chinese read it straight down, but Japanese read it according to Japanese grammar, hence necessitating reading by going back and forth.

Fan Ts'ieh—The mode of giving sounds to a character in Chinese dictionaries by furnishing initial consonant with one known character and the vowell and ending with another known character.

Furigana—Kana alongside Kanji to show how to read.

Fifty Sounds—Same as Gojuh-in.

Gojuh-in—(Literally: fifty sounds)—The name given to the arrangement of kana characters in phonetic order beginning with five vowels and nine different consonants, each of which combines vowels.

Go-on—(Literally: Wu-sound)—Sound of Chinese characters, Japan learned from Chinese during Wu dynasty of China.

Hentai-gana—Hiragana in variant forms, much used during pre-Meiji era.

Hepburn System—A system of Romaji introduced by Dr. J. C. Hepburn in his dictionary of Japanese language published in 1872.

Hiragana—A kind of kana, see under kana.

Honji—(Literally: real character)—Chinese character with correct manner and number of strokes. Chinese characters generally are also known as Honji in contrast to kana.

Ideograph—Same as Chinese character.

Ideographic Script—Same as Chinese character.

In—Same as "on."

I-ro-ha—The name given to the arrangement of kana characters in order of a poem supposed to have been composed by Kohboh Daishi. I-ro-ha is the first three letters of the poem.

Japanese Orthography—Rules of using kana correctly.

Japanese Sounds of Kanji—Sounds given to Chinese characters by Japanese, according to the meaning in Japanese language. (Same as kun, yomi or reading). Also, "on" or "kun" as used by Japanese.

Japanese Syllabary—Same as kana. So named because kana consists of a vowel or consonant followed by a vowel. The only exception is n, which may precede or follow a vowel.

Japanese Sounds—Sounds in Japanese speech. Also sounds given by Japanese to Chinese characters.

Japanese System of Romaji—Ramaji based on written kana, in contrast to that of Hepburn system, which is based on sounds of Japanese language.

Jion-Kanazukai—A branch of Japanese orthography, which treats of correct use of kana in expressing sounds of characters.

Kana—(Literally: provisional name) — Japanese syllabary much simpler than Chinese characters, each having only one definite sound, although in combination some sounds change according to the rules of Japanese orthography. There are two kinds of kana, namely: "Katakana" and "hiragana." Katakana is derived from a part of Chinese character used phonetically. Hiragana is a further abbreviated form from the grass style of writing of character used phonetically.

Kanbun—Same as classical Chinese.

Kaeriten—Marks indicating how to read classical Chinese in order of Japanese grammar.

Kanamajiribun—A sentence or composition written with Chinese characters and kana mixed in reading order.

Kanazukai—Same as Japanese orthography.

Kanji—(Literally: Han-character)—Same as Chinese character.

K'anghi Tsz'tien—(Literally: K'anghi dictionary)—The name of standard Chinese dictionary, compiled during Ts'ing dynasty.

Kan-on—(Literally: Han sound)—Sound of Chinese characters, prevalent during Han dynasty. The greater part of sounds of Chinese characters learned by Japanese belongs to Kan-on.

Katakana—A kind of kana. See under kana.

Koji—(Literally obsolete character)—Chinese character the form of which is out of date.

Kojiki—(Literally: Records of ancient matters)— Earliest Japanese publication dated 712 A.D. contains mythology and earliest history of Japan. Written in Chinese mixed with Kanji used phonetically.

Kokugo Kanazukai—A branch of Japanese orthography which treats of correct use of kana in Japanese language.

Kuan Hua—(Literally: official discourse)—Same as Mandarin Chinese.

Kun—(Literally: meaning)—Meaning in Japanese language, attached to a Chinese character.

Mandarin Chinese—Chinese dialect of north of Yang Tsz' River, now used as the official language of China.

Manyoh-gana—Chinese characters used phonetically in Japan, i. e., Chinese characters employed to write Japanese language, by making use of a sound value only, regardless of inherent meaning of characters.

Man-yoh-shuh—(Literally: book of milliard leaves) —An anthology of the most ancient poems of the Japanese language. Dated about 760 A.D.

Min-on—(Literally: Ming-sound)—Sounds of Chinese characters, Japan learned from Chinese of Ming dynasty.

Norito—Shintoh rituals written with Chinese characters used literally and phonetically.

On—(Literally: sound)—Sound of Chinese characters, as learned by Japan from China originally. It is invariably monosyllabic in China, but in Japan final consonants aside from n or ng are followed by another vowel making dissyllable in such instance.

Pre-Meiji Era—Time before the Meiji restoration (1868), when Japan opened doors to the world commerce.

Reading—Same as yomi.

Romaji—Alphabetical transcription of Japanese language.

Romaji Systems—Hepburn and Japanese systems of Romaji.

Romanized Kana—Romaji representation of kana characters.

Romanized Japanese—Same as Romaji.

Ryakuji—Chinese character in abbreviated or contracted form, mostly used in hand writing.

Seiji—(Literally: correct character)—Chinese character with correct manner and number of strokes, i. e. the same as the first meaning of Honji.

Shing—(Literally: voice)—Peculiar mode of intonation or breathing of Chinese sounds by which Chinese distinguishes fine shades of sounds hardly possible for foreigners to master or even to imitate. Japanese generally never acquired enough of shing to introduce it into their language.

Shin-on—(Literally: Ts'ing sound) — Sounds of Chinese characters, Japan learned from Chinese of Ts'ing dynasty.

Shintoh—(Literally: the ways of the Gods)—Mythology and ancestor and nature worship of

Japan, existed before the introduction of Buddhism into Japan, and which still continues to exist in a modified form.

Stress—Accent on words (the sense in which it is used in this work).

Toh-on—(Literally: T'ang sound)—Sounds of Chinese characters. Japan learned from Chinese of T'ang dynasty.

Wakun—Same as Kun.

Yomi—(Literally: reading)—Same as Kun.

Zokuji — (Literally: vulgar character) — Chinese character the form and strokes of which are in popular use but regarded to be incorrect by learned people.

WORKS CONSULTED

Sacred Books and Early Literature of the East
Enzyklopaedisches Woerterbuch ....Muret-Sanders
Modern Philology ....Dwight
Life and Growth of Language ....Whitney
Principles of Speech ....Bell
Japanese Etymology ....Imbrie
Primer of Phonetics ....Sweet
Elements of French Pronunciation ....Broussard
Notes on Syllabic Consonants ....Bell
Sounds of R ....Bell
Faults of Speech ....Bell
Webster's International Dictionary
Standard Dictionary
Century Dictionary
Encyclopedia Britannica 9th, 11th, 14th editions
Encyclopedia Americana
French Pronunciation and Diction ....Jack
Things Japanese ....Chamberlain
Gile's Dictionary of Chinese Language
漢英韻府 ....Williams
作文講話 ………………………………芳賀 杉谷
字　源　……………………………　簡野道明
國字問題十講 ………………………　加茂正一
日本文典 ……………………………　大槻文彦
ローマ字獨げいこ ………… 田中館 芳賀 田丸
現代書法論 …………………………　圓道祐之
言語學概論 ……………………　安藤正次
日本及日本國民之起源 ………… 小谷部全一郎
草書實習法 ………………………　井上靈山
萬葉歌百首講義 ……………………　木村正辭
發音學 ………………………　遠藤隆吉
古事記新講 …………………………　次田　潤
中朝事實 ………………… ……　山鹿素行
草書字典 ……………………… ……　圓道祐之
新古今集選釋 ………………… 佐佐木信綱

For Product Safety Concerns and Information please contact our EU
representative GPSR@taylorandfrancis.com
Taylor & Francis Verlag GmbH, Kaufingerstraße 24, 80331 München, Germany